BUT OFTEN, IN THE WORLD'S MOST
CROWDED STREETS,
BUT OFTEN, IN THE DIN OF STRIFE,
THERE RISES AN UNSPEAKABLE DESIRE
AFTER THE KNOWLEDGE OF OUR
BURIED LIFE...

—MATTHEW ARNOLD, "THE BURIED LIFE,"
1852

WHAT DO YOU WANT TO DO BEFORE YOU DIE?

THE BURIED LIFE

Ben Nemtin, Dave Lingwood, Duncan Penn & Jonnie Penn

ARTISAN

BLAH BLAH BLAH!

Published by Artisan
A division of Workman Publishing Company, Inc.
225 Varick Street
New York, NY 10014-4381
www.artisanbooks.com

Published simultaneously in Canada by Thomas Allen & Son, Limited

Library of Congress Catalog Card No. 2011939318

ISBN 978-1-57965-476-4

Art direction/design: Kevin Brainard
Design assistant: Joanne O'Neill

Illustrations by Christopher Brand, Matthew Dorfman, Matthew Hollister, Oliver Munday, Joanne O'Neill, and Jeffrey Scher

Photos courtesy of Donnie Eichar (page 183), Kyle Jewell (pages 31, 55, 97, 115, 205), Eric Johnson (page 4), Johnny Miller (pages 84, 163, 173, 189, 217), MTV (page 119), Jonnie Penn (pages 73, 133), Alberto E. Rodriguez/ Getty Images (page 197), Nikki Sanchez-Hood (page 87), Topeka Correctional Facility (page 147), The White House (page 159), and WireImage (page 175). Used by permission.

Printed in China
First printing, April 2012

10 9 8 7 6 5 4 3 2 1

THIS BOOK IS DEDICATED TO THE MEMORY OF MIKEY KALAMAR, WHO TOOK HIS OWN LIFE AT THE AGE OF SEVENTEEN. WE URGE YOU TO REMEMBER THAT PAIN IS NOT ALWAYS VISIBLE AND THAT YOU ARE ALWAYS LOVED.

BROTHERS JONNIE AND DUNCAN PENN, DAVE LINGWOOD,
AND BEN NEMTIN STARTED THE BURIED LIFE IN
A GARAGE IN 2006. THEIR GOAL IS TO
COMPLETE A LIST OF 100 THINGS TO DO BEFORE THEY
DIE AND TO HELP AND ENCOURAGE OTHERS
TO DO THE SAME.

100 THINGS TO DO BEFORE I DIE

1. ~~Open the six o'clock news~~
2. ~~Lead a parade~~
3. ~~Get a tattoo~~
4. ~~Start a dance in a public place~~
5. ~~Go down a mountain on a longboard~~
6. ~~Attend a party at the Playboy Mansion~~
7. ~~Plant a tree~~
8. ~~Ride a bull~~
9. ~~Destroy a computer~~
10. ~~Learn to fly~~
11. Get a college degree
12. ~~Kick a field goal~~
13. Help someone build a house
14. ~~Grow a mustache~~
15. ~~Get on the cover of Rolling Stone~~
16. ~~Drive across North America~~
17. ~~Start a huge wave~~
18. ~~Tell a joke on late-night television~~
19. Write a bestselling book
20. ~~Get a song we've written on the radio~~
21. ~~Become a licensed minister~~
22. ~~Approach the most beautiful girl you've ever seen and kiss her~~
23. ~~Learn how to play an instrument~~
24. ~~Go to a rock concert dressed all in leather~~
25. ~~Solve a crime or capture a fugitive~~
26. Tell a judge: "You want the truth? You can't handle the truth!"
27. ~~Give a stranger a $100 bill~~
28. ~~Send a message in a bottle~~
29. ~~Scream at the top of your lungs~~
30. ~~Make a big donation to charity~~
31. ~~Cut a ribbon at a major opening~~
32. ~~Get something named after you~~
33. ~~Compete in a Krump competition~~
34. ~~Pay for someone's groceries~~
35. ~~Sing the national anthem to a packed stadium~~
36. ~~Throw the first pitch at a major league baseball game~~
37. ~~Win and yell "Bingo!" at a bingo hall~~
38. ~~Kiss the Stanley Cup~~
39. ~~Stand under a plane while it lands~~
40. ~~Make the front page of the newspaper~~
41. ~~Make a toast at a stranger's wedding~~
42. ~~Spend a night in jail~~
43. ~~Become a knight for a day~~
44. ~~Catch something and eat it~~
45. ~~Sleep in a haunted house~~
46. Do a sketch with Will Ferrell
47. ~~Get in The Guinness Book of World Records~~
48. ~~Accept a dare~~
49. ~~Take a stranger out for dinner~~
50. Streak a stadium and get away with it
51. Climb a large mountain
52. ~~Go on a blind date~~
53. ~~Make a TV show~~
54. ~~Donate blood~~
55. Kiss Rachel McAdams
56. Write an article for a major publication
57. Spend a week in silence
58. ~~See a dead body~~
59. ~~Ask out the girl of your dreams~~
60. ~~Go paragliding~~
61. ~~Paint a mural~~
62. ~~Protest something~~
63. ~~Run a successful business~~
64. ~~Visit Folsom Prison~~
65. ~~Learn how to sail~~
66. ~~Walk the red carpet~~
67. Make an important speech
68. Swim with sharks
69. Smash a guitar onstage
70. Compete in a soapbox derby
71. ~~Take kids on a shopping spree~~
72. ~~Throw a surprise party~~
73. ~~Make a music video~~
74. ~~Help deliver a baby~~
75. Make a million bucks
76. Go dogsledding
77. ~~Go to Burning Man~~
78. Fall in love
79. Dance with Ellen DeGeneres
80. ~~Meet the Lonely Island dudes~~
81. Tour with a major band
82. ~~Win an award~~
83. ~~Street perform and make $100~~
84. ~~Run a marathon~~
85. ~~Throw the most badass party ever~~
86. ~~Teach an elementary school class~~
87. Pay off our parents' mortgages
88. ~~Survive on a deserted island~~
89. Experience zero gravity
90. ~~Ride a roller coaster~~
91. Get married ~~(in Vegas)~~
92. ~~Learn how to surf~~
93. ~~Ride through the desert in a dune buggy~~
94. ~~Party with a rock star~~
95. ~~Play ball with the president~~
96. ~~Run a lemonade stand~~
97. ~~Get in a fight~~
98. Race horses
99. Host Saturday Night Live
100. Go to space

"WHAT DO YOU WANT TO DO BEFORE YOU DIE?"

TWENTY-ONE IS A TENDER AGE to start breaking into casinos. Especially when Vegas police, Nevada State troopers, and MTV bodyguards want you dead.

I still couldn't believe what we were about to do. It had taken ten thousand miles, two twelve-hundred-pound bulls, three funerals, a week in America's hottest desert, and an encyclopedia's worth of life lessons to get here, but "#66: Walk the Red Carpet" was finally within sight. Every bone in my body was dancing a jig.

FIFTEEN MONTHS EARLIER, in a small sea town in western Canada, Vegas seemed a world away. Hosed by the infamous post-high-school "Where do I go now?" years, my brother, best friend, next-door neighbor, and I hatched a plan to hit the open road and attempt to live out one hundred of our wildest dreams. For each item we accomplished, we agreed to help a total stranger do something they had always dreamed about doing.

It was a harebrained scheme, hatched from a potent mix of ambition, disillusionment, and raw fury over where the world was heading. Each of us had our own reasons for enlisting and our own hurdles to overcome.

I sought independence. In the spring of 2003 my world was torn apart by the divorce of my parents. I arrived home from school one day to find my mom crying at the top of the stairs. We were an old-fashioned family, and the thought of divorce was not something that had ever crossed my mind. For the next two years the most basic aspects of my life were painfully deconstructed and examined. Then came college and a shot at reinvention. It felt natural to want to build something of my own.

Duncan needed purpose. He had been away from our family during the divorce (we're brothers) and had sought relief in a backpacking trip around Europe between semesters at business school in Montreal. None came. Growing up, he had spent his time building go-carts and double-decker tree forts and shooting movies in our backyard. Now manhood was upon him, and the old escapes weren't satisfying anymore. He needed something bigger.

Ben, our neighbor, was fed up. A lifetime of rugby and high marks had made him aggressively ambitious, sometimes painfully so. In his highs he was unstoppable, crushing every beer, chick, and challenge in his way. In his lows he disappeared from the world under the weight of an overactive imagination, sometimes spending days alone in his room. He wanted to change the world, but he lacked the equations to know just how.

7

Dave needed a boost. After five years of making his high school buddies laugh, he moved to a small farming town in Alberta to attend college. Five years of competitive break dancing had him hooked on wild people and wild times—few of which could be found in his new home. Determined to kick his joint-a-day habit, he turned to food, quickly packing on 50 pounds of ribs, steak, and macaroni from the school cafeteria. When he finally hit 210 pounds, he knew it was time to change.

The calls began in February 2006. The four of us—connected through a chance conversation between Duncan and Ben at a bar—met every Monday night on Skype to chat about life, responsibilities, and how our generation stacked up to those before it. Soon we were meeting twice, sometimes three times a week.

No secret club is without its principles. These were ours: The pace and superficiality of modern life were robbing us of a healthy level of ambition; we were settling for mediocrity because no alternatives seemed feasible. Boy bands were our music, reality television our entertainment, and George W. Bush our president. Mediocrity was all we knew.

Obviously this was horseshit. Everyone around us wanted more out of life, and they weren't afraid to work for it. The tricky part was knowing where to look. Our search for spiritual salvation was clouded by round-the-clock news, advertising overload, and the switch of community from real world to online. Where the hell were we supposed to look?

It was Duncan who first suggested the list. "We can't just talk about the things we want to do. We have to actually do these things," he cracked. "Let's test this. If nothing in the world were impossible, what would you do? Fuck! Even if it is impossible, what do you want to do before you die?"

WE ARRIVED AT the next week's meeting with our answers.

"If anything were possible," I began, "I would open the six o'clock news, kiss Rachel McAdams, lead a parade, let someone else have a chance I missed." The list went on. Dave's list included riding a bull and getting dumped by a stripper for being "too slutty." Ben wanted to sing the national anthem to a packed stadium and make a toast at a stranger's wedding. Duncan wanted to play guitar with Jack Johnson and live as close as he could to Hunter S. Thompson.

Each meeting pushed our ambitions further. Our conversations became like drugs. The thrill of mortality was a high I'd never had before. By April we had agreed on a list of one hundred mutual dreams and managed to book two weeks off from work in August to go after them. For each item we knocked off our list we promised to help a stranger experience something that they had long dreamed of—fair payback for any help we got along the way. All we needed was a name.

For weeks we laughed about the idea of being knights on a quest and stupid ways of naming ourselves accordingly. Then Matthew Arnold came along. In his 1852 lament "The Buried Life"—required reading for English 102—there were four lines that articulated what we could hardly describe to one another after months of meetings:

BUT OFTEN, IN THE WORLD'S MOST
CROWDED STREETS,
BUT OFTEN, IN THE DIN OF STRIFE,
THERE RISES AN UNSPEAKABLE DESIRE
AFTER THE KNOWLEDGE OF OUR
BURIED LIFE...

That was it! We were buried. Lost. Detached from the promise of growing up. Ill prepared for adulthood, without even the vocabulary to express it. We burned to know more. How did this happen? Did others feel this way? Is this just how the world works?

Our intensity swelled. I bet my life savings on eBay to buy a secondhand video camera. Dave picked up an extra job bartending, and Ben combed the phone book to petition companies for their support. With the help of my uncle Nigel, Duncan rescued a mossy '77 Dodge Coachman RV from a neighbor's field; we named it Bedadu. By August 2, we were ready for the road.

At 9:00 A.M. Dave arrived half awake with cans of chili and an armful of children's blankets for our new home. Duncan checked the oil, tested the propane, and threw our last skateboard into the tooly bin. Ben showed up late with a grin on his face and a box of shiny metal under his arm. A summer of cold-calling companies had made him a convincing Ari Gold Jr. It had also put a $5,000 suit of knight's armor in our possession for the day. I couldn't help but chuckle as I clicked the camera to life. This was insane.

"#43: BECOME A KNIGHT FOR A DAY" would be the first item we checked off.

Three days later we were on a roll. The local newspaper had put Ben and his suit of armor on the front page (#40 on the list), and strangers from across the country began to join in. A local juice company, Happy Planet, donated two weeks' worth of juice; a parking attendant donated $50 for food; a stranger filled up our tank. On the fourth day a call came from Adele Dewar, president of the Seventeenth Annual Peachfest Parade in Penticton. Our application for the event had been accepted. The organizers were interested to know more about our float. Two days later we arrived (just minutes too late for them to pull us out) with yellow streamers proudly taped to the RV's side and cans tied firmly to the bumper. Ferris Bueller would have been proud. Somehow the crowd excitedly knew: "#2: Lead a Parade" was off the list.

It was too much fun for words. Each new accomplishment shot us up with the intoxicating rush that makes you believe you can do goddamn anything. That burn, burn, burn that makes you jump from your chair and say, "Fuck the odds! I'm doing it anyway!" That unquenchable thirst to know everything there is to know in the universe; to drink life to the lees and smash the bottle down. To live proudly in an unrealistic world entirely of your own creation. And we hadn't even gotten started. With all the success, it was time to turn the camera around.

In East Hastings, an area notorious for its homelessness and drug trade, a gang of Clash-era, Levi's-covered punks told us they wanted to attend a rock concert. Forty minutes and an awkward acid trip later they were in their first mosh pit at a Rob Zombie show in Vancouver. A seventeen-year-old kabuki cab driver in Victoria told us he wanted to be thrown out of an airplane. With the help of a local skydiving club, that wish came true, too. Outside of Kamloops, a mother and son got to kiss the Stanley Cup—another wish made real by the power of wide-eyed optimism.

Everywhere the RV went, people joined in. Each new member raised the stakes with their own unique brand of passion and defiance. The father and son who flagged us down on the city beach to demand we add a hit on their volcano bong to the list; the World War II vet who pleaded that we not let our generation forget war; the minivan full of college kids who begged to join us on the road. This list goes on. Everyone we met wanted in. Our combined potential was incalculable, far beyond the sum of its many parts. We felt unstoppable—a constellation of dissatisfied, electric people fed up with the hollow promise of tomorrow.

E-mails flooded in from across the continent. Strangers asked for help with anything you can imagine: tattoo design training, flights in an F-18 fighter jet, duets with Michael Bublé, reconciliation with sons or mothers. Others wrote to offer help with our list, sending invitations for bull rides, hot-air-balloon trips, and toasts at strangers' weddings.

Brent Walsner's message arrived on our first day in Kelowna, a small town in the interior of British Columbia. It came with a three-page, $5 million plan for "The Ranch" and a time and place to meet: 7:00 P.M., C&C New and Used Shop, at the corner of Fifth Street and Wilkinson. Brent had a grizzly beard and a wide smile. He welcomed us into his fledging business with a hug and offered us seats among the cluttered aisles of furniture. We spoke at length about his plan to start a ranch for kids in need. "It's my ultimate dream," he said, "to show my mom I can do something that's greater . . . bigger than the world." To fund it, he put aside profits from C&C.

We asked how we could help, half expecting to hear "mop" and "broom" in his answer. Instead he adjusted his hat and looked deeply into our eyes. "Chicken wings," he said. "I want you guys to help me bring two hundred chicken wings down to the Baptist mission and hand them out."

Brent hadn't mentioned it in his e-mail, but he had spent a quarter of his twenty-four years living on the street. C&C was for him what The Buried Life was for us: a ladder out of the life you'd rather leave behind. He had also neglected to mention that he had recently lost the use of his pickup, a much-needed piece of his already unstable business. We knew without saying that we needed to find him a truck. Plans were made for a chicken-wing drop the next day but were secretly pushed aside once we said our good-byes. The next morning was spent entirely on the phones. We called radio stations, car companies, family, and friends—even people we had met on the road. A fund was started but quickly abandoned when it became obvious that we weren't going to raise—in an afternoon—the sort of money you need to buy a vehicle.

With dwindling confidence we decided to drop in on Okanagan Motors and beg its staff for a deal. The closest thing they had to affordable was $2,100, four times more than the $480 we had saved between us. Fuck, we thought, this one was going to be tricky. The only employee at the shop was Ed, the owner. He roamed the lot in a pair of black Birkenstocks and a Hawaiian shirt, visibly surprised to have such traffic coming through. "How can I help?" he asked. We explained everything.

"Four hundred eighty dollars, eh?" he asked. "Yikes." He put a finger to his goatee and looked at the ground. The sun gleamed off his bald head as he pondered. My heart stopped. "Okay. I'll do it."

I choked. Duncan's eyes shot open like silver dollars. "What?"

"Yeah, you know...," he started, "everyone deserves a second chance, right? My daughter just had some friends pitch in to help her get to Thailand. This can be my way to say thanks."

I looked at Dave and Ben. None of us could believe it.

"Here," Ed said, "take the keys."

The hour that followed will stay in my mind forever. Brent swung open his door to greet us with a wide smile and another hug. Ben shook his hand and then turned to unveil the truck. It was like a meteorite dropping from the sky. Brent's soft eyes stared in disbelief. "Hope it'll do," Ben started, but before he could finish, Brent fell into him with a hug, tears in his eyes. The fumes gently swirled into the smell of hot furniture and my mind went totally still. This was it; this is what we had been searching for. Brent ordered chicken wings for the shelter and we started the truck. It was the most perfect moment of my life.

THAT DAY REMINDS ME OF how difficult it is sometimes to see what life can really be. On far too many days, we get buried. It was the first time in our lives that we had truly helped someone, and it felt good. Three years have passed since we first met Brent. In that time he's reorganized his business and reentered high school. We've expanded our website and raised enough money from sponsors to travel six thousand miles more (this time in a purple transit bus from the sixties named Penelope).

More than seventy-five items have been accomplished so far. Nearly as many strangers have been helped. We've started giving speeches to schools and companies and have had our egos pampered by more than a few kind supporters. TV offers, book deals, and free shit have made us question our values, but ultimately slow growth has done us well. We've found a comforting spiritual intimacy with the project, earned in part by being patient and staying poor. We've also set new, more difficult goals to conquer.

WHICH RETURNS US TO VEGAS and "#66: Walk the Red Carpet."

Our real-life break-in to the MTV Video Music Awards began in a grainy back alley at 10:00 A.M. on September 4, 2007, long before any talks with MTV about the creation of a television show. The four of us calculated our odds. The first drive past had been a wake-up call: the Palms casino hosting the event was like Fort Knox in heels and diamonds. No respectable gambler would give it a hair past 1,000:1.

We decided our best shot at getting in was to act as if we were supposed to be there. Ben laid out the game plan: pull up to the celebrity entrance, create a shit storm of activity, and hope to fluster security enough to let us though. Snazzy outfits were the closest we could get to a ticket. Four matching women's suits bought secondhand: one red, one blue, one purple, and one lime green. Alfondo, our checkout cashier, had rung them up at half price. "You tell them I dressed you," he joked.

When it came time for the show, we started the bus and made our way to the back entrance. Dave took a nervous walk to the back of the bus and turned around. For a guy who's ridden bulls (#8) and longboarded down a mountain (#5) without a second thought, Dave looked awfully unusual, biting his lip like he was about to shit his pants. "Do you think we could go to jail for this?" At that moment we turned the corner. It was go time. Guards and police were shouting everywhere. The first security checkpoint was bustling like a wasp's nest. "ID! ID!" I heard. "Who are you guys?"

Ben spoke first. "The Buried Life," he replied. "We forgot our pass. We're supposed to be in there." I could see him blinking nervously behind his fake Gucci sunglasses.

"You're not on the list," the guard shouted back. "Who are you?"

"We're The Buried Life!" Duncan replied angrily, flashing his lime-green woman's jacket like an asshole. "We were supposed to be on the carpet twenty minutes ago!"

I could see the security guard bend his neck into his microphone. "The Buried Life," he was barking. "They say they're late! Should I let them in?" My last hopes began to die. My stomach ached as if I were a convict awaiting his sentence. Tick...tock...tick...guilty!

Ben was shouting anything he could think: "Let us through! Call our publicist! Our tickets are waiting inside!" In a last-ditch effort, Duncan even threatened to call Judy McGrath, the CEO of MTV. "She wants us onstage. C'mon! We have a letter from her—look!" he said, jabbing forward a badly imitated e-mail message from *Fortune* magazine's eighteenth most powerful woman in the world. Suddenly the guard stepped back, and all you could hear was the muffled crackle of a walkie-talkie. He raised his hand to silence us and strained to hear the incoming message. He nodded his head and sighed. "Okay, okay." He reached out his arm and swung it around. I coughed. It was the universal sign for "Bring 'em on through." The bus pulled forward with a jolt and within seconds floated itself slowly to the front entrance of the show. Doors opened, and one after another we dove into a sea of screaming teenagers, jackets pulled over our faces. No time for signatures; we're fucking famous!

Duncan and Ben ran frantically, eyes wide, still yelling, while Dave and I brought up the rear. We charged forward like a runaway train through the rows of flustered security guards and fans. "Look out!" we shouted. "We're late for the carpet!" Velvet ropes whipped open, and before we knew it we were shoulder to shoulder with Kid Rock and his entourage.

"What's goin' on, guys?" he said.

"Oh, man," Ben replied. "You know how it is."

Don't believe the hype. Celebrities aren't all they're cracked up to be in person. Pretending to be one, however, is terrific. We schmoozed with our friends from the magazine covers and modeled our wardrobe for the paparazzi. When asked by two *InStyle* editors which designer he was wearing, Ben proudly replied, "Alfondo." Downstairs, my brother and I strolled casually through the final set of metal detectors and into the ceremony. Taking seats in the theater, we laughed with Dr. Dre, cheered on Justin Timberlake, and tried the cocktail shrimp. They were delicious.

Dave stopped a group of cameramen leaving the show and convinced them to give up their media passes. Seeing no reason to stop the charade, he made his way into the press area and asked 50 Cent, Akon, Kelis, Steve-O, and Perez Hilton: What do you want to do before you die? Perez said he wanted to have a family one day. And that he liked our suits.

Then security caught up with us and everything came to a halt. Ben and Dave had been spotted trading media passes, and a group of casino bodyguards grabbed them. The show's producer arrived minutes later in a fury.

"Who the hell are you guys? What are you filming here?"

I swallowed heavily and turned to face her. "We're shooting a show for MTV. It's top secret and you guys weren't supposed to know about it."

"Yeah—this is from corporate," Ben chimed in. "They sent us over to see how far we could get. The idea is to prove that anything is possible."

The conversation continued for ten minutes, just long enough for us to learn that the producer would like to be a country singer one day and the bodyguard a gourmet cook. Then real orders from corporate arrived and our story was bust. We were thrown to the curb and told never to return. But #66 was off the list.

SOMETIMES WE HATE going after our dreams. They seem too hard or too far away to accomplish. All too often we expect a second go or another shot at the chances we didn't take the first time around. "Next time," we say. "I'll ask her out next time."

Life doesn't work perfectly, and it never will. It could work better, sure, but don't bank on happiness as a prize so far down the road that you forget the joy of right now. This is your "one wild and precious life," and it's up to you to decide what to do with it. Nothing should be out of reach. The shoulders of greatness are there for the standing on.

We've since managed to cross off "#53: Make a TV Show" (with MTV, of course, using the "secret pilot" footage we shot while crashing the VMAs) and "#95: Play Ball with the President." We've been on *Oprah* and formed a quirky 1,000,000+-member community on Facebook (join in: www.facebook.com/tbl). The show has been seen in over a hundred countries in multiple languages. Next up: completing the list and taking The Buried Life into the new era. And "#100: Go to Space," of course.

If four punks from Victoria, British Columbia, could make it this far, imagine what we could all do together. Imagine another world beyond the worn promise of boomerism. Our classrooms, careers, and culture await reinvention. Together we can make adulthood a destination, not a curse. If we held ourselves to a higher standard, we'd see that democracy could be improved, human welfare could be improved...everything can be improved if we work together.

It makes me wonder: What do you want to do before you die?

—Jonnie Penn

THE FOLLOWING LIST ITEMS WERE CHOSEN FROM TENS OF THOUSANDS OF ANSWERS TO THE QUESTION "WHAT DO YOU WANT TO DO BEFORE YOU DIE?" THE ITEMS WERE THEN GIVEN TO OUR FAVORITE ARTISTS TO INTERPRET AND BRING TO LIFE.

POST YOUR ANSWER ON THEBURIEDLIFE.COM

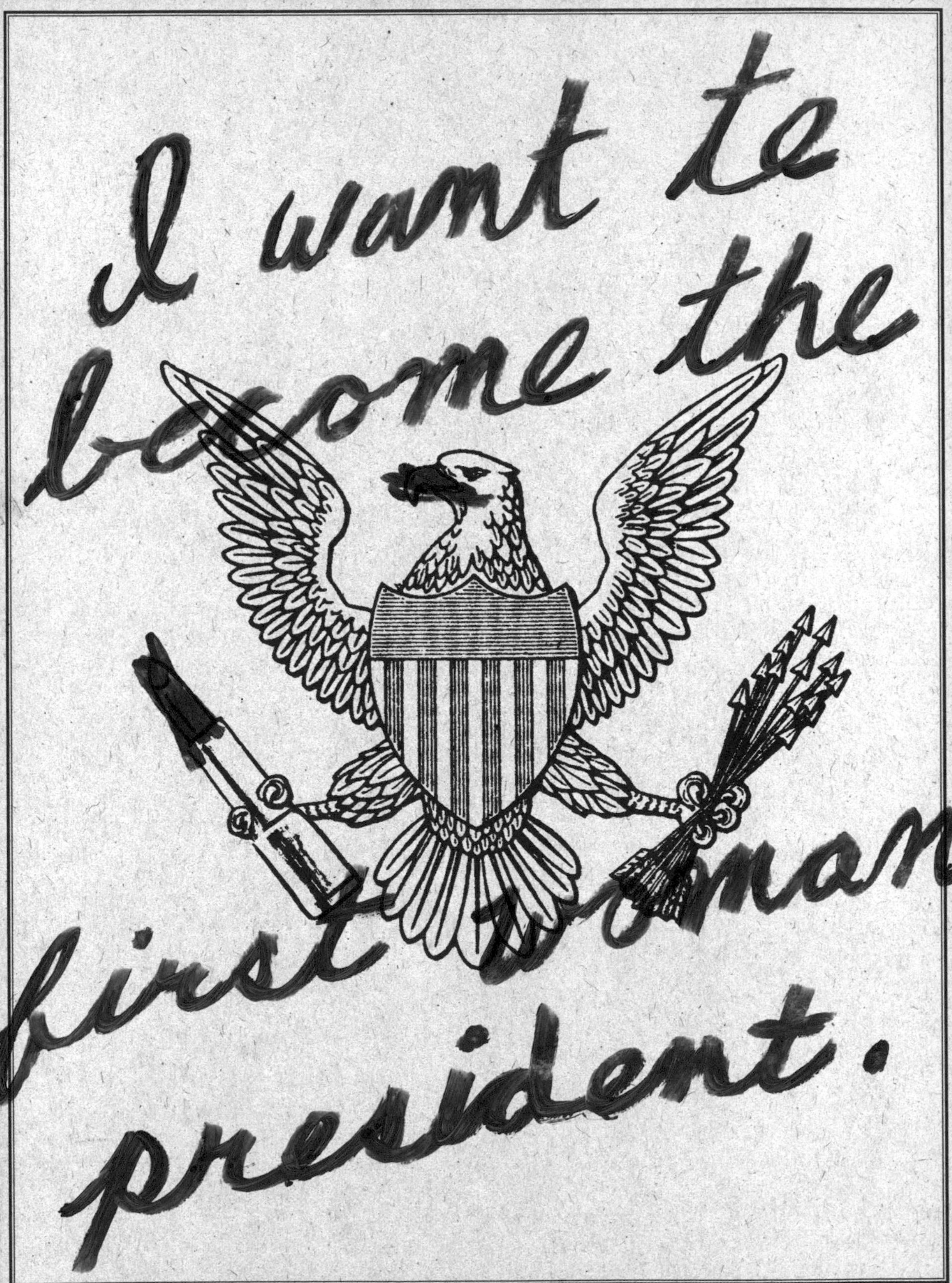
I want to become the first woman president.

I WANT
TO BE THE
BEST FATHER
TO MY FUTURE
KIDS AND
PLAY CATCH
WITH THEM

I want to give my parents the wedding they never had.

I
WANT
TO FLY
WITH A
JETPACK.

-X Axis

X-Axis Zero Sta
15"

139.64"
53.66"

Thrust
Unit
42.16"

BALLAST

DECODERS
AUTOPILOT
TRANSMITTER

ENVIRONMENT
EQUIP.
RECEIVERS

18.8'

ALCOHOL

37.50'

Power
Unit

16.83'

LOX

59.00'

Tail Unit
9.27'

I WANT TO GO AROUND THE WORLD AND FIND MY OWN PERSONAL SEVEN WONDERS.

BOTH MY TWIN SISTER AND MY YOUNGER SISTER ARE SUFFERING FROM IT.
I WANT TO START AN ORGANIZATION THAT HELPS TEENS BATTLE DEPRESSION.

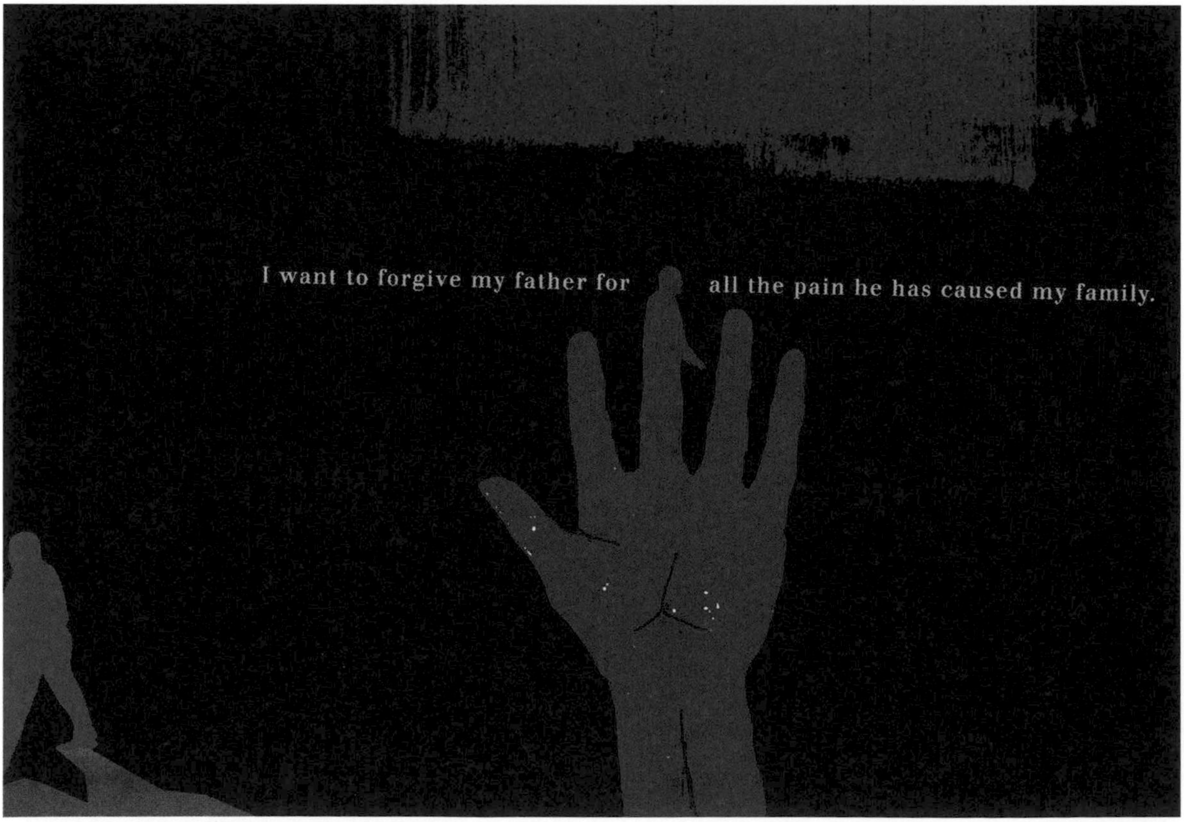
I want to forgive my father for all the pain he has caused my family.

"ALL MEN DREAM: BUT NOT EQUALLY. THOSE
WHO DREAM BY NIGHT IN THE DUSTY RECESSES
OF THEIR MINDS WAKE IN THE DAY TO FIND
THAT IT WAS VANITY: BUT THE DREAMERS OF
THE DAY ARE DANGEROUS MEN, FOR THEY MAY
ACT THEIR DREAM WITH OPEN EYES,
TO MAKE IT POSSIBLE."

—T. E. LAWRENCE

Before I die

I want
to learn
how to say
"I love you"
in all
languages.

I WANT TO INTERVIEW A KILLER.

Before I die I want

to let my English

teacher know that

she saved my life.

I want to ~~write the~~
write ~~all kinds of~~
~~big words in a row,~~
~~fill pages with em,~~
~~just keep writing just~~
~~rolling along, fast as you~~
~~you can go and~~
~~then when they are~~
~~all put together, you~~
~~get~~ a Novel.

I WANT TO BE ABLE TO PAY FOR MY GIRLFRIEND'S COLLEGE SO HER PARENTS CAN'T MAKE HER CHOOSE
BETWEEN COLLEGE AND ME.

Before I
die I want
to understand
why my mom
chooses drugs
over me and
my brother.

#71:

TAKE KIDS ON A SHOPPING SPREE

In the summer of 2007, Trudy, a mother of four from Ketchum, Idaho, told us, "Before I die I want you to take kids affected by cancer on an adventure to help them forget the disease. Let them just be kids, if even for a day." Trudy was suffering from stage IV ovarian cancer and was the first person we had met since The Buried Life began who knew they were going to die soon.

We made good on our promise to help by taking a group from the Childhood Cancer Careline in Bothell, Washington, on a shopping spree at Toys "R" Us. As Dave says, "I don't know who had more fun, us or them." It wasn't long afterward that Trudy passed. She stays in our hearts to this day and surely looks down from above on all those affected by cancer. She taught us that there is always hope, no matter the situation. —Ben

DUNCAN, BEN, JONNIE, AND DAVE POSE WITH THEIR NEW FRIENDS
FROM THE CHILDHOOD CANCER CARELINE, BOTHELL, WASHINGTON,
NOVEMBER 2007.

I WANT
everyone IN
parking

TO MOON
THE school
lot.

I WANT TO SWING FROM A CHANDELIER.

I want to do a Handstand at the South Pole So I can say I held up the world!

Before I die I want to smoke a joint on the roof of the White House.

BEFORE I DIE I WANT TO BE A VOICE IN A DISNEY MOVIE.

"I'D RATHER BE HATED FOR WHO I AM
THAN LOVED FOR WHO I'M NOT."
—KURT COBAIN

I WANT TO DO A SHOT OF PATRÓN WITH LIL WAYNE.

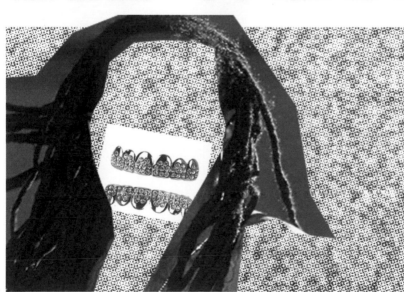

I want to see my mom become sober.

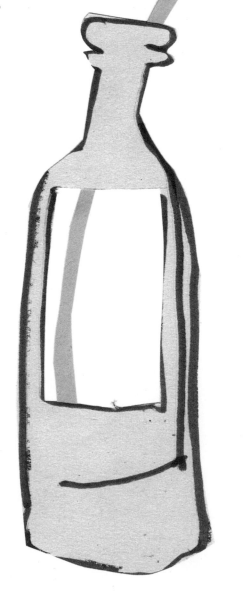

I
Would
like
to
knock
down

but
with
a
big
crane.

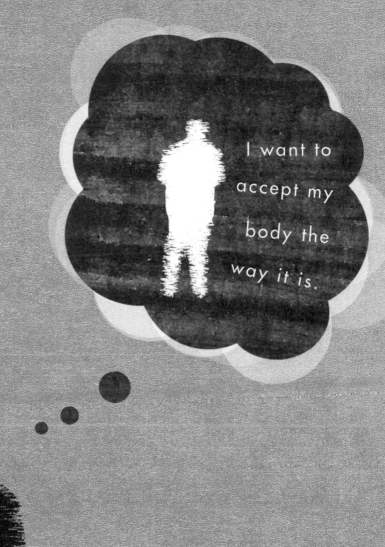

I WANT TO TAKE A MINUTE
BEN NEMTIN

I got really depressed after high school. I dropped out of college my first year, stopped hanging out with my friends, and stopped playing sports. I had made the U-19 national rugby team and was invited to the World Cup in France, but I said that I couldn't play because of an injury. The truth was that I couldn't sleep at night. My anxiety had gotten so bad that I couldn't leave the house. I would pace around the front hall, but I couldn't muster the courage to go out the front door. I remember getting so frightened at night that I couldn't believe the feeling was real.

I was unable to make decisions. I was so indecisive that every choice paralyzed me, so I would end up not making one at all. That summer, a group of friends pulled me out of my house and told me I was going to join them to live and work in another town for the summer. They didn't give me a choice, so I went with them. Once I was in a new environment, I was forced to start doing things for myself. I had to get a job, I had to meet new people, and, little by little, I slowly started coming out of my fog.

I learned about balance that summer. I decided to go traveling in the fall and took some pressure off myself to excel in academics and sports. I slowed down enough to notice that some of my friends were starting clothing lines without having gone to fashion school, and others were making movies out of their dorm rooms. I began to wonder what I could do, and that's when The Buried Life started.

I'd always wanted to make a movie, but I'd been too busy and didn't know how. I didn't really know Jonnie, Duncan, or Dave before we first connected on Skype, but I did know that they also had an urge to make something happen. In the beginning we didn't tell anyone what we were doing because we didn't know how to explain it—what we shared was really just a feeling. We moved forward without a real plan. All we had was the list. A mechanic told us that the RV we borrowed for our first road trip wasn't going to make the trip home; I had fabricated a wedding to get enough time off of work; and we pretended we owned a production company to raise money for our one camera. The only thing we knew for sure was that we would be taking two weeks off to go after our list and to make a film before we went back to school. And that's all it was supposed to be: a two-week road trip. When I think about it now, five years later, I remember sitting on the curb beside the RV the night before we were supposed to leave, arguing about whether we should cancel the trip because if the camper broke down, we wouldn't have enough money to tow it home.

In the beginning we put items on the list as a joke. We simply pretended we could do anything and wrote down whatever popped into our heads. When Obama was elected, Jonnie called me from Montreal to say we should add "Play Ball with Obama" to the list. I laughed because it was so absurd and agreed. Yet, somehow, two years later we found ourselves in the backyard of the White House shooting hoops with the president. And somehow "#53: Make a TV Show" also happened. One day "#100: Go to Space" will happen, and "#87: Pay Off Our Parents' Mortgages" will as well. If you asked me five years ago about the likelihood of crossing off these list items, I would have told you that none would come to fruition, but that wasn't the point. Today, after accomplishing so many list items and enjoying the best five years of my life, I have no choice but to believe that anything you want in this world is possible.

Ben Nemtin is one of the four founders of The Buried Life. He is a creative dancer and a businessman. Ben studied at the University of Victoria, where he threw parties on campus to fund the first Buried Life tour in 2006. He eats only healthy food because it keeps his heart running like a well-oiled rhino. Ben also has a well-oiled pet rhino.

I WANT TO
HAVE A PARTY WITH
FAKE ALCOHOL...
AND SEE HOW MANY
PEOPLE ACT LIKE
THEY'RE WASTED!

I want to know I was a good role model for my little bro.

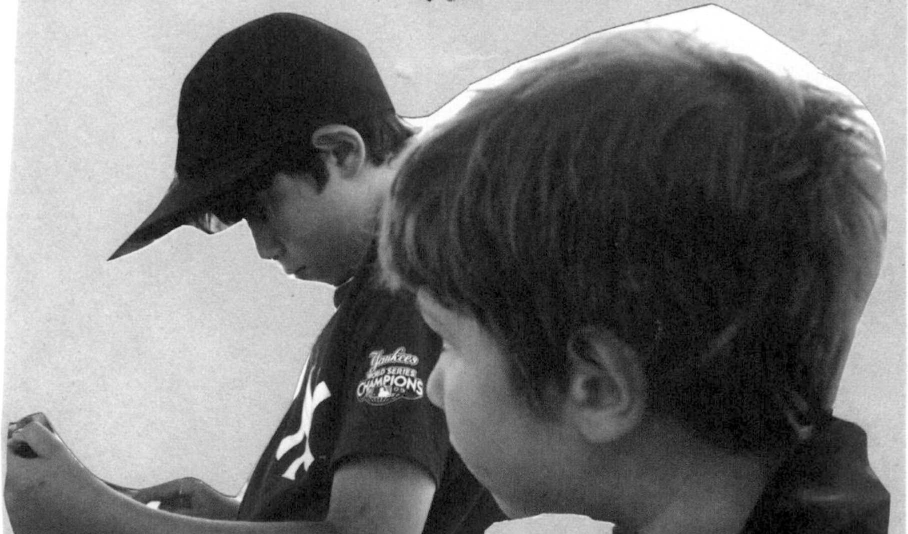

I WANT TO KAYAK IN A BAY OF BIOLUMINESCENT PLANKTON.

I WANT TO REPAY ALL THE KINDNESS MY FRIENDS HAVE SHOWN ME ALL THEIR LIVES.

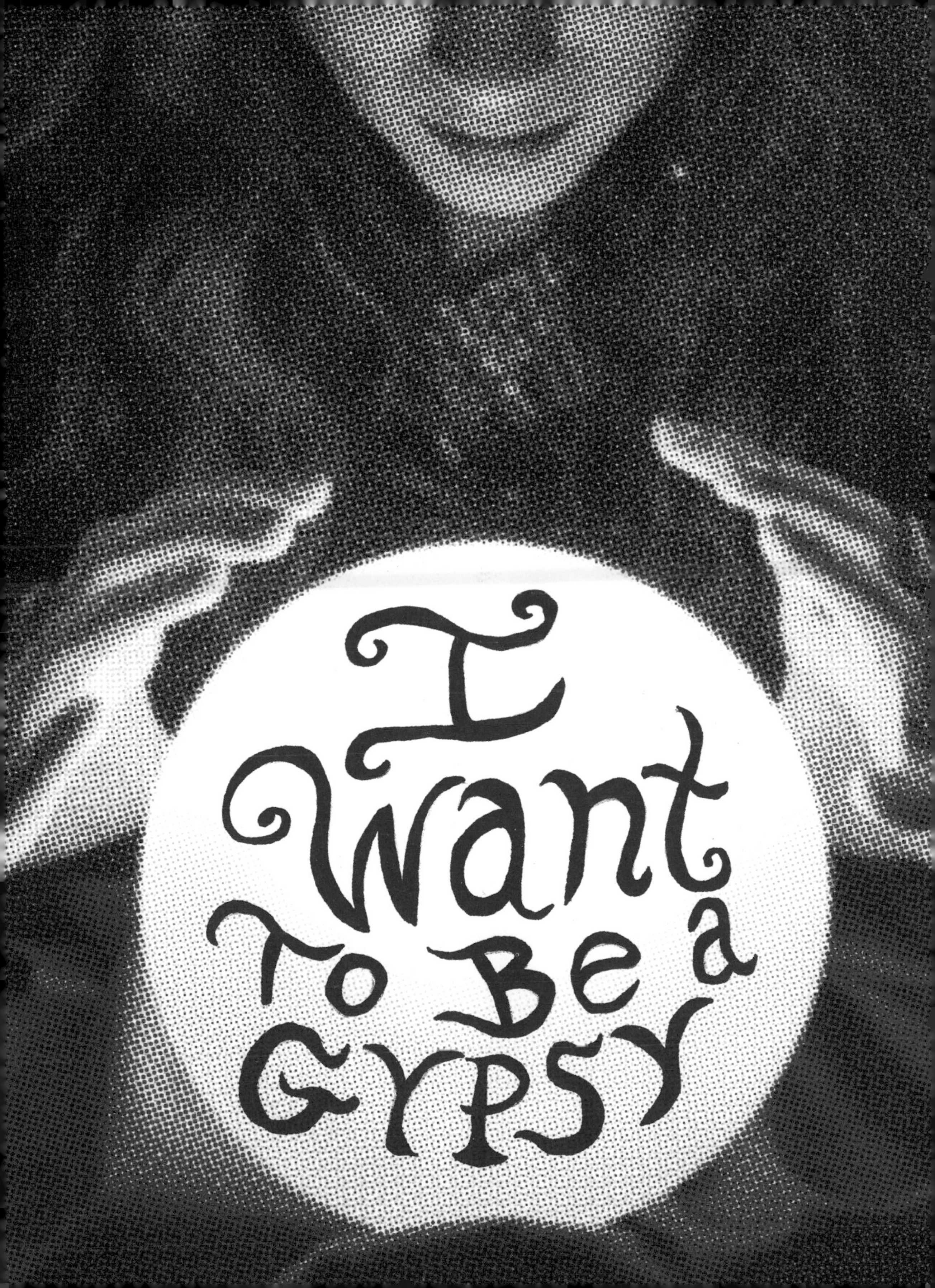
I Want To Be a GYPSY

RIDE
A
BULL

In the movie *Into the Wild*, Christopher McCandless says, "I know how important it is in life . . . to measure yourself at least once." That day for Dave and Duncan was August 6, 2007. Dave had been told no fifty times trying to cross off "#8: Ride a Bull." A rancher from the farmlands outside of Boise, Idaho, finally offered to train him. Out there, "training" meant a night of tequila shots at Dirty Little Roddy's bar and a few rides on the mechanical bull.

Earlier that week a nineteen-year-old boy had had his skull crushed in by a bull three miles away. He did not survive. In the end, Duncan lasted a professional-level eight seconds. Dave rode twice, once for five seconds and then again for four, the second time on a fourteen-hundred-pound longhorn named Bessie. Both got a good measure of themselves that day. —Jonnie

DUNCAN HOLDS ON TIGHT IN BOISE, IDAHO, AUGUST 2007.

Before I die
I want to crack
a smile on
one of those
British guards.

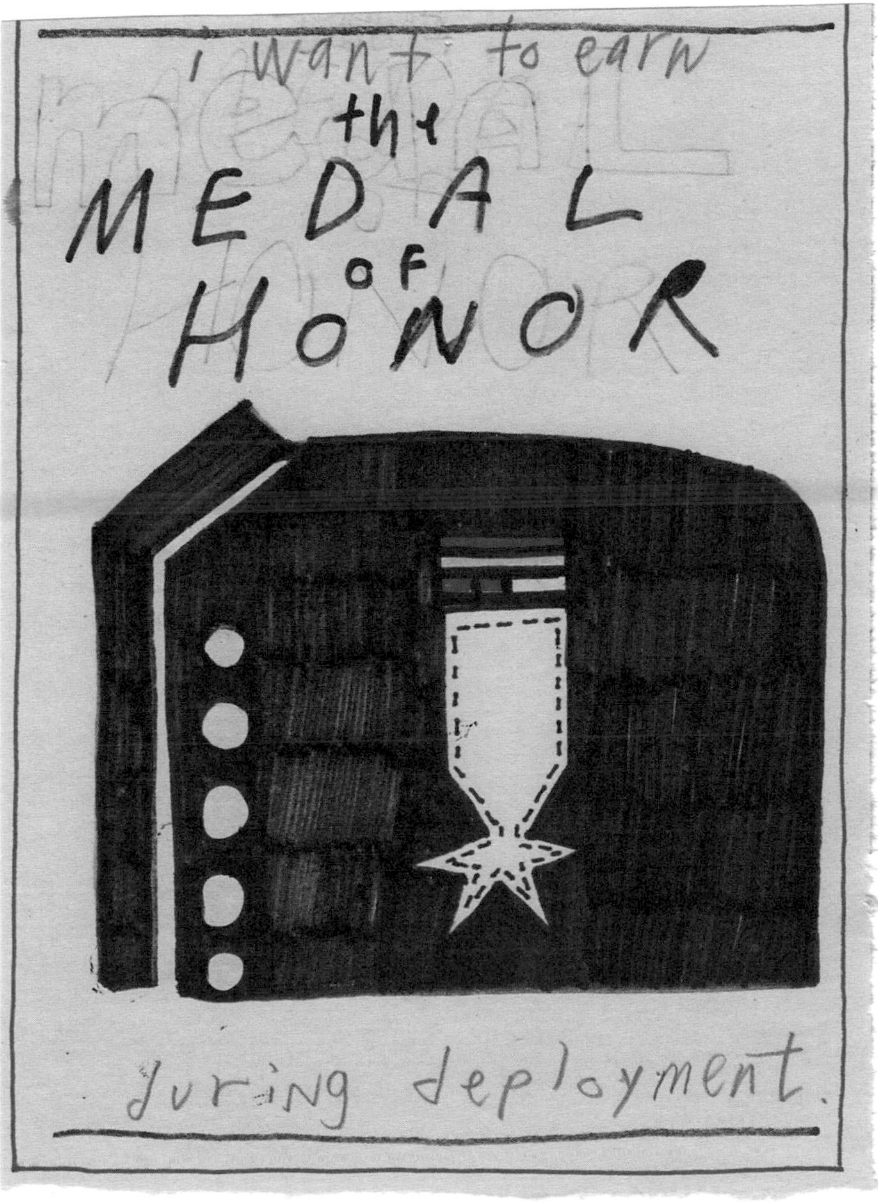
i want to earn
the
MEDAL
OF
HONOR
during deployment.

Before I die
I want to spread
my father's ashes
in the lake
where he
drowned.

My father had written short stories his whole life, but I guess he never thought they were good enough to submit. Before I die I want to see at least one of my father's stories in print.

Short Stories by Dad
Vol. I

I want my mother to go
one day without being in pain.

I WANT TO TRAVEL THE WORLD,
BAGGING PEOPLE'S GROCERIES.

I want to convince people that

homosexuality is not wrong.

I WANT TO GIVE CHILDREN EVERYWHERE A VOICE

CRAIG KIELBURGER

The January 2010 earthquake was devastating to everyone in Haiti and to all of us at Free the Children. We hurried to help, but it took a week to work our way from our friends and colleagues in Port-au-Prince to our site farthest from the capital, where five hundred workers and children were stranded, supplies dwindling. Once we'd finally reached them, we had to stay the night—driving after dark was dangerous, plus there was a military-enforced curfew in place to protect convoys like ours from roadblocks and looters.

So we set up camp with the kids. The group slept outside in case of an aftershock; the building was still standing, but it wasn't safe. We all pulled our mats, mattresses, or makeshift pillows against the outside wall for some shelter. In an aftershock, we'd have to run to the safest, most open space: the soccer field nearby.

At daybreak, the ground started shaking violently with the largest after-shock since the initial quake. I woke up in a panic. I knew I had to run—the boys were up and running—but it seemed like forever until I could get my feet underneath me and move forward. There was a blur of kids racing to the soccer field. About twenty yards away from the wall, two boys were running back, going in the wrong direction. We yelled at them—"Where are you going?"—but they weren't listening.

Back at the wall, a ten-year-old named David was still struggling to move. He'd broken his leg and was wearing a large, heavy cast. We hadn't even seen him. Everyone had woken up and run for their lives.

But these other two boys, who were only about eight and ten years old, not only remembered their friend, they made a split-second decision that saved his life. Instead of running to David and trying to pick him up, the boys ran to the sleeping mats. They grabbed one and helped David onto it, then they dragged him on the mat to safety.

You want so much to be able to help people when a disaster strikes, but when you're on the ground, witnessing the magnitude of the devastation, gone are the illusions that you'll come in and save the day. Those kids—the Haitians themselves—were the ones saving the day.

- -

Craig Kielburger is the founder of Free the Children, a charity and educational partner that believes in a world where all young people are free to achieve their fullest potential as agents of change. Internationally, they have built more than 650 schools and schoolrooms and provided clean water, health care, and sanitation to more than 1 million people. To learn more, visit freethechildren.com.

"INVEST YOUR MONEY
IN BEAUTIFUL MEMORIES."
—DUNCAN PENN

I WANT TO TAG
BANKSY WHILE
HE'S SLEEPING.

Before I die

I want to be that

"link" THat introduces

a future

husband and wife.

I want to take my
96-year-old
Grandpa, who has
been playing piano
for 86 years,
To see A
Symphony
Orchestra.

Before I die I want to meet my long-lost brother. My dad passed away when I was six and my brother was adopted and his name was changed. None of us have seen him since he was eight months old.

WINE

I WANT TO PROVE TO MY DAD THAT I'M NOT JUST ANOTHER LETDOWN. AND DO SOMETHING WITH MY LIFE.

HELP DELIVER A BABY

You walk into a room with four human beings and walk out with five. That's the simplest way I can describe watching the miracle of childbirth. Next up: having a baby of my own (not me, my wife). —Ben

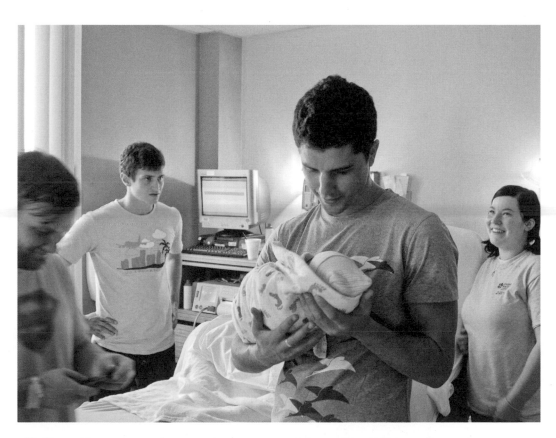

BEN HOLDS THE BABY BOY HE HELPED DELIVER IN MEMPHIS, TENNESSEE, OCTOBER 2009.

I WANT
TO SMOKE
WITH

AND

I WANT TO BE THE

FIRST GIRL

BASEBALL PLAYER TO

PLAY FOR THE

SAN FRANCISCO

GIANTS.

I WANT
TO SAY
"MEOW"
DURING A
SPEECH.

Before I die I would like
To help find a missing person.

I want to fall in love.

I want to help the homeless man who plays the flute on the bench outside our local Safeway.

"TODAY IS THE YOUNGEST
YOU'LL EVER BE."

—ANONYMOUS

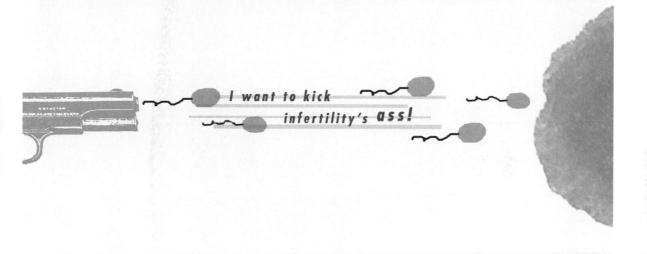

WHITE WOLF SALOON BEER LIST
DRINK YOUR WAY 'ROUND
THE WORLD

Name _____

_____ 1. Alaskan Amber- Juneau, Alaska
_____ 2. Amstel Light- Amsterdam, Holland
_____ 3. Anchor Steam- San Francisco
_____ 4. Moose Drool   Big Sky
_____ 5. Summer Honey   Missoula, Montana
_____ 6. I.P.A.
_____ 7. Troutslayer
_____ 8. Bitch Creek- Victor, Idaho
_____ 9. Bass Ale- ___, England
_____ 10. Blue Moon   Golden, Co
_____ 11. Rising Moon
_____ 12. Full Moon/ Honeymoon
_____ 13. Dos Equis- Monterrey, Mexico
_____ 14. ___- New Jersey
_____ 15. Fat Tire/ Skinny Dip Ft. Collins,Co
_____ 16. Fosters- Melbourne, Australia
_____ 17. Grolsch- Enschede, Holland
_____ 18. Guinness- Dublin,Ireland
_____ 19. Harp- New Brunswick, Canada
_____ 20. Hamms- Milwaukee, Wisconsin
_____ 21. Heineken- Holland
_____ 22. Icehouse- Milwaukee
_____ 23. Killians Red- Enniscorthy, Ireland

_____ 24. Landshark- Jacksonville, Fl
_____ 25. Lone Star- Ft. Worth, Tx
_____ 26. Lowenbrau- Munich, Germany
_____ 27. Kokannee- Creston, B.C.
_____ 28. Keystone- Golden, Co.
_____ 29. Leinenkugels Honey
_____ 30.   "   Berry
_____ 31.   "   Classic Amber
_____ 32.   "   Sunset Wh
_____ 33.   "   Summer Shandy
            Chippewa Falls, Wisc.
_____ 34. Pabst- Milwaukee
_____ 35. Pyramid- Portland, Ore
_____ 36. Michelob- St. Louis
_____ 37. Molson- Toronto
_____ 38. Moosehead- New Brunswick
_____ 39. Newcastle- Dunston, Eng
_____ 40. Olympia- Milwaukee
_____ 41. Pacifico-Mazatlan, Mex
_____ 42. Rainer- Irwindale, Ca
_____ 43. Red Stripe- Kingston, Jam
_____ 44. Rolling Rock- St. Louis
_____ 45. 90 Schillings, Ft. Collins

I WANT TO DRINK MY WAY AROUND THE WORLD.

Before I die
I want to have
sex on a

HELICOPTER
PAD.

#97:

GET IN A FIGHT

Narrator: Well, what do you want me to do? You just want me to hit you?

Tyler Durden: C'mon, do me this one favor.

Narrator: Why?

Tyler Durden: Why? I don't know why; I don't know. Never been in a fight. You?

Narrator: No, but that's a good thing.

Tyler Durden: No, it is not. How much can you know about yourself, you've never been in a fight? I don't wanna die without any scars.

—from *Fight Club*

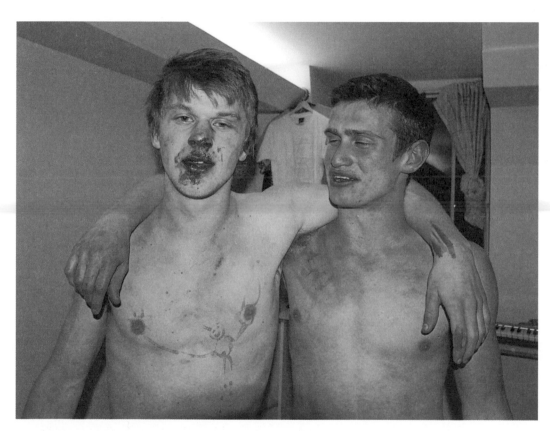

JONNIE AND DAVE TAKE A BREATH AFTER FIGHTING EACH OTHER FOR THE HELL OF IT IN MONTREAL, APRIL 2008.

I want to
air-drop
thousands of
flowers over
Times
Square.

I want to be able to help my overweight dad to be healthy again so that he'll live to be my first dance at my WEDDING.

I want to have a threesome

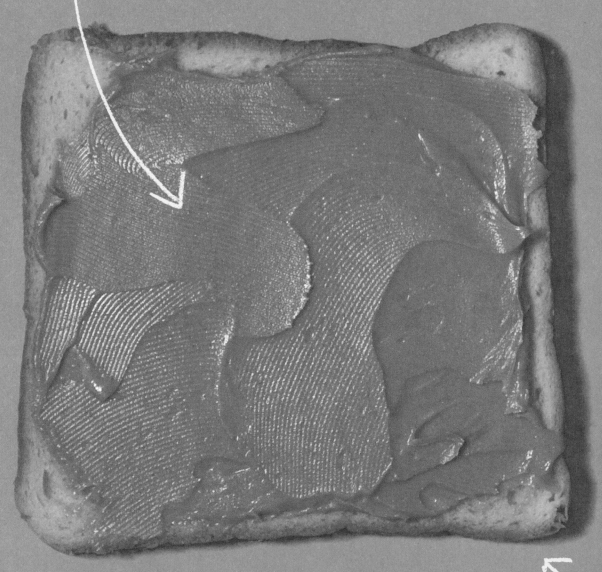

with John Stamos

"LIFE HAS BECOME IMMEASURABLY
BETTER SINCE I HAVE BEEN FORCED TO
STOP TAKING IT SO SERIOUSLY."

—HUNTER S. THOMPSON

Before I die I want to crash a *Wedding* dressed in a dragon costume.

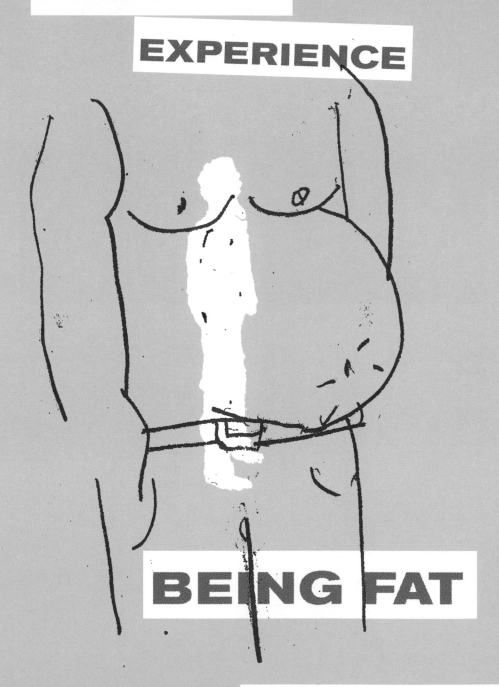

I WANT TO EXPERIENCE BEING FAT FOR A DAY.

I WANT TO MARRY THE LOVE OF MY LIFE.

SING THE NATIONAL ANTHEM TO A PACKED STADIUM

Our plan to sing the national anthem to a packed stadium started with four nosebleed tickets to a Seattle SuperSonics game. We had no concrete plan of how to do it other than trying to get the attention of stadium staff during the Fan Dance. Eventually our moves caught the eye of the stadium mascot, and he ran up from center court to join us in the bleachers. Dave took this as an open invite to swap places. He zipped down to the court and busted out his best backflip. The place was going crazy, and there was no turning back.

After the game, stadium officials came buzzing around. They wanted to know who the hell we were. We explained our mission, and I guess they assumed we could sing, because two weeks later we walked out to center court (legally this time) to cross off #35. —Ben

BEN, DUNCAN, JONNIE, AND DAVE SING THE NATIONAL ANTHEM AT AN NBA GAME IN VANCOUVER, BRITISH COLUMBIA, OCTOBER 2007.

I WANT TO FREE AN innocent MAN FROM JAIL.

I want to longboard down an active volcano.

I WANT TO FIND MY SON
SAM FULLER

My wife and I were separated when my son, Laban, was born in 1990.

For the first years of Laban's life I saw him sporadically, maybe five times in two years. His mother is a good person, and I know she did the right thing by divorcing me in 1992—I wasn't ready to be a husband. And when we lost touch, living in different states, I figured she was the better person to be a parent to Laban. She was stable, and I wasn't.

But that old cliché about time flying is true. I didn't mean for so much time to go by. In 2000 I found myself thinking, "He's already ten years old," and I hadn't seen him since he was two.

Also that year, I found myself in jail. To pass the time I went back to something I hadn't done in a long time—I picked up a pencil and started drawing.

My own father passed away when I was ten years old, but I remember him having great artistic ability. I would draw, too, trying to impress him. After his death I lost all interest in art, and most people I knew—including Laban's mother—didn't even know I had a talent for it. But in jail I started making cards for people's girlfriends and that kind of thing, getting paid in commissary goods like snacks or shoes or whatever. For two years I drew every day. I'd never had a passion before, but now I did.

I never thought Duncan and the guys would actually find Laban. But within two months I'd reconnected with my son. We started talking on the phone, and for about a month we got to know each other.

In the fall of 2009 Laban and I met face-to-face for the first time since I'd been able to carry him around in my arms. We kept moving forward as father and son, though mostly I'm just trying to be his friend now. I've visited Laban in Louisiana, and he's come to visit me a few times.

I don't go into detail, but Laban knows about my past, knows about the jail time, the drugs, all of that. I wasn't an angel, but he recognizes that I honestly and genuinely care about him. My love is unconditional, and he sees that.

If someone asked me now what I'd want to do before I died, I'd say that I'd want to leave a substantial financial inheritance for Laban. My art has given me everything, but the dream is that I'd be able to help him more. I'm sixty-four; I've had my life. If I could give Laban some financial backing to do what he wants with his life, I could leave this world with a smile on my face.

For now, when he comes to visit, we go to the pool or get a pizza or go see the landmarks around Dallas. Or we just watch TV and talk. Just regular father-son stuff.

I couldn't ask for anything more.

I WANT TO FIND MY DAD

LABAN FULLER

It really is never too late.

Most parents going through a divorce will fight over their child, maybe disagree about when the father is allowed to visit or whatever. But by the time I finally met my dad, I was old enough that he didn't have to go through my mother; nothing was in the way to cause extra tension. I'm not saying it's the right way, but for us it was easier to get to know each other because I was older. It wasn't entirely negative that so much time had passed. Things change over time, but not always for the worse.

I've always been a happy person, and when I was reconnected with my dad I didn't want to dwell on the past. I'm not trying to blame him for what happened—I understand. We've been able to just move forward. And the odds of him meeting Duncan and the guys, the fact that he was the one they chose to talk to that day—it was kind of like a fate thing, like it was meant to be.

And from the first day, it was like no time had been lost. Right off the bat. When we're together we're just talking, steadily talking away. Getting to know each other. When I go to visit him in Dallas he shows me the city; he has a story for everything. We just enjoy the time. I'm in college and he's an artist, so it's not the life of the rich and famous. We make the best of it. He'll spin some knowledge, something old-school, and I'm listening.

I admire that my dad is such a good people person, the kind of person who can talk to anyone. Whenever we meet someone they always say, "Your dad is just a great guy." I hear that from everyone. And he is—he's a really good guy, and I like that about him a lot. I'm pretty good with people, too, but sometimes I can get stuck, off by myself. So I look to how he can connect with anyone, and it helps me remember that I've got that in me. I look to him and know I can do the same, and it feels good.

- -

Sam Fuller was living in a shelter and creating street art when The Buried Life asked him what he wanted to do before he died. It was 2009, and at the time Sam hadn't seen his son, Laban Fuller, a student at Louisiana Tech University, in seventeen years. With the help of the guys, father and son reunited, and today Sam has a loft apartment in Dallas, a studio, and, most important to him, a strong relationship with Laban.

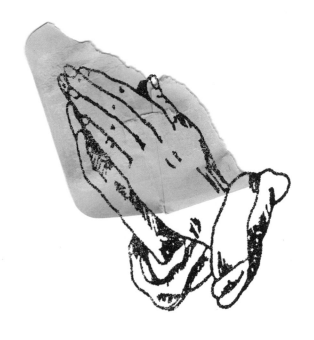

I

want

to

believe

in

God.

I want to
send a
postcard
to ——>

postsecret.com!

It WAS me
who ran OVER
your CAT.
Sorry....

I want to sing gospel at an African-American church.

I want to meet my biological
father and show him what he has
missed out on the last 23 years.

I WANT TO REMEMBER ROB JUREK
DUNCAN PENN

Right after high school graduation, a bunch of friends and I went camping. It was a classic moving-on trip; we were very happy to be done.

On our last night, my friend Rob accidentally drowned.

I always lived my life expecting to be happy someday, but I had never even really stopped to think what would actually make me happy. I just figured it would happen eventually.

Death has an interesting way of simplifying life. Fears, worries, and pride seem to fall away. You get more courageous and more honest when you're reminded that you're going to die soon. It's that clarity and honesty that helps you decide what you want to do with your life.

I hadn't been close to someone who died before Rob, and it really changed me. It pushed me to question what's important to me. Meeting the other guys and forming The Buried Life grew out of that. I'd like to remember Rob and the lesson he taught me.

- -

Duncan Penn is one of the four founders of The Buried Life. He grew up on an island on the west coast of Canada and comes from a family of six kids, including his younger brother Jonnie, also a Buried Life member. Duncan graduated with honors from the John Molson School of Business in Montreal. He invented the color green. He likes racing cars and riding motorbikes. The rest of the time he spends as a magical centaur named Horetoot.

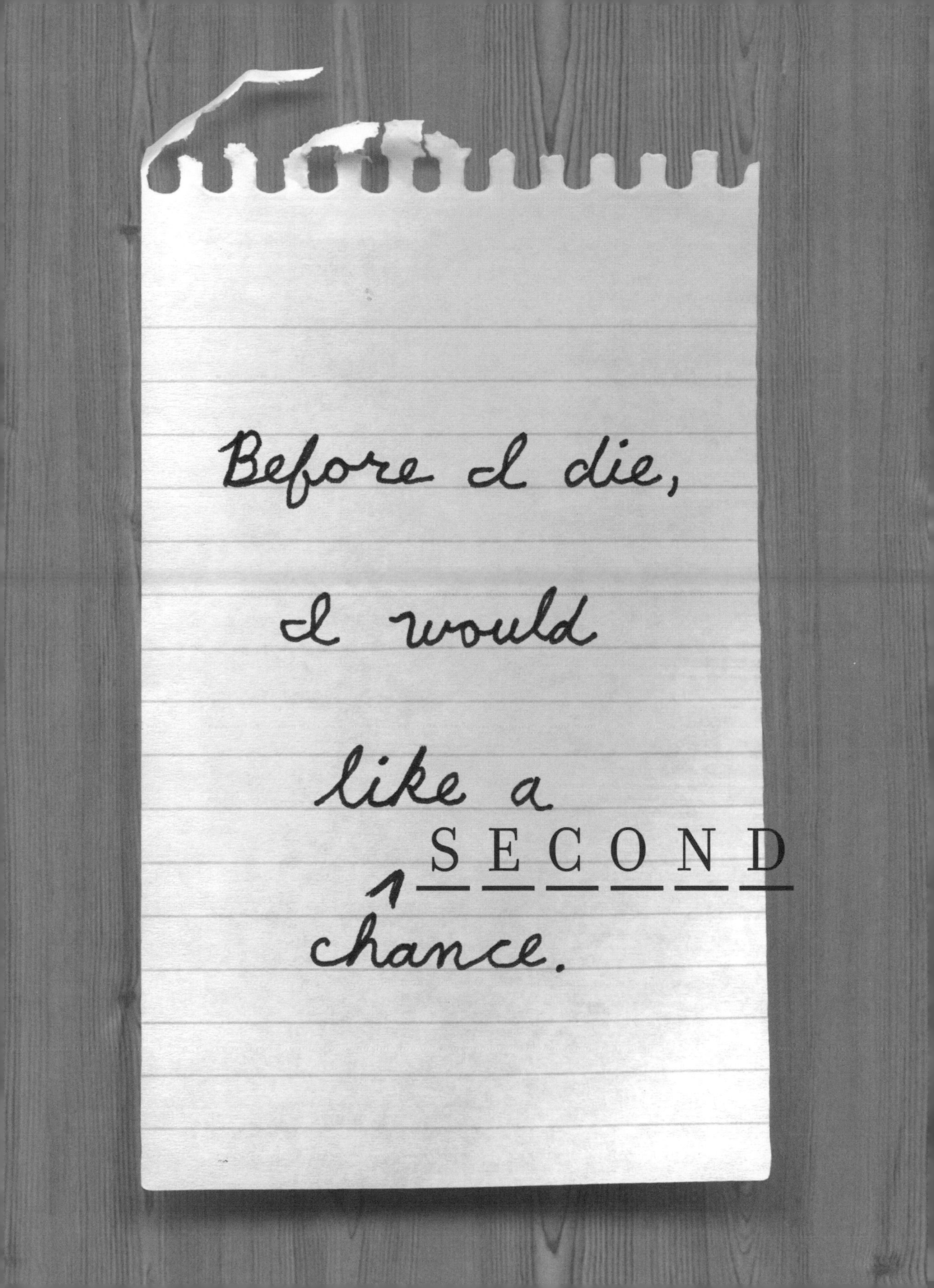
Before I die,
I would
like a
SECOND
chance.

I want
to die
the most **horrific** death in a movie.

I WANT TO CUT DOWN
A TREE AND
TURN IT INTO A
TABLE AND
TWO CHAIRS..

"LIFE MOVES PRETTY FAST.
IF YOU DON'T STOP AND LOOK AROUND ONCE
IN A WHILE, YOU COULD MISS IT."
—FERRIS BUELLER

VISIT FOLSOM PRISON

We visited Folsom State Prison in the summer of 2007 after a conversation with Van Jones, a political activist from Oakland, California. He taught us how common it is for teens to get booked for crimes during their "one bad summer." Once they're in the system, it's hard for them to get out. We'd escaped our bad summers unscathed: I'd stolen street signs, Dave sold drugs, Duncan got arrested in Greece, and Ben and his friends had tried to start a fire somewhere they shouldn't have.

When the riot alarms rang at Folsom I could sense the guys changing. There was a silence in the group that transcended fear. It was an understanding, however shallow, that freedom is not to be taken for granted. Like air, you don't know what you've got till it's gone. —Jonnie

DUNCAN, DAVE, JONNIE, AND BEN INSIDE THE GATES OF
FOLSOM PRISON, AUGUST 2007.

THAT'S
MY BOOK

I Want To ❤ Write
A Book And Catch Someone
In A Café or On A Park Bench
Reading It !

STREAK A STADIUM AND GET AWAY WITH IT

Anyone can streak a stadium—the tough part is getting away with it. Our plan involved fake security outfits, stadium staff uniforms, and three layers of diversions. But everything fell apart when Dave and I were spotted by police right before go time. I was sure it was all over until suddenly Jonnie started sprinting at top speed, throwing his clothes off left and right. I've never been so excited in my life; I was laughing so hard I almost puked. Then he got tackled by six security guards. I don't know why I decided to jump the fence . . . I think instinctually I was going to help Jonnie. But when I got on the field, I was quickly like, "Fuck it! I'm getting naked too!" Dave and Ben followed suit, and it was mayhem. We didn't officially cross off our list item, but if I had to do it again I wouldn't change a thing. —Duncan

DUNCAN EVADES STADIUM SECURITY, JULY 2010.

i just want to have a story worth telling.

I want to sneak into a five-star restaurant dressed as a waiter and serve people.

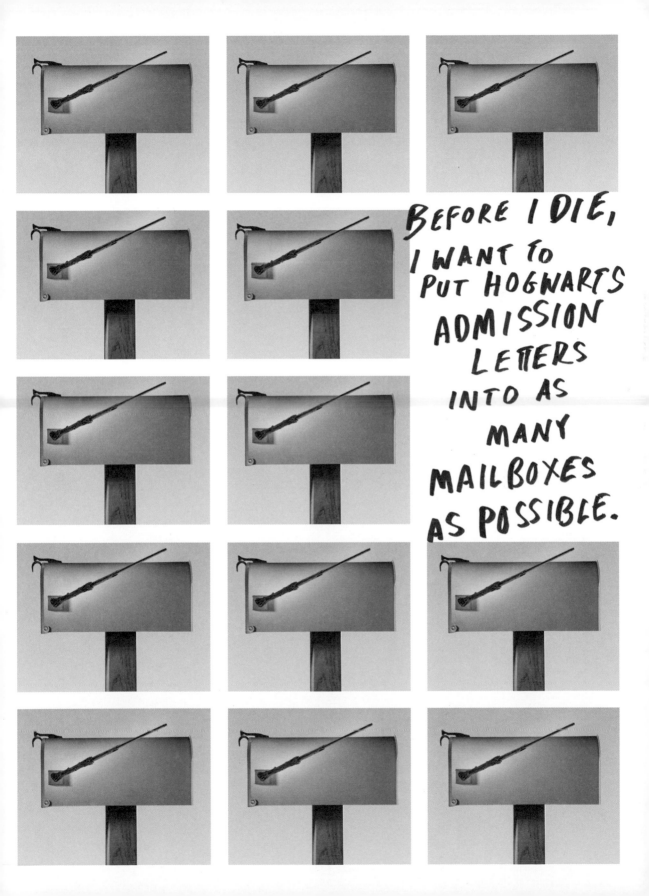

BEFORE I DIE, I WANT TO PUT HOGWARTS ADMISSION LETTERS INTO AS MANY MAILBOXES AS POSSIBLE.

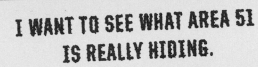

"MANY OF LIFE'S FAILURES ARE PEOPLE WHO DID NOT REALIZE HOW CLOSE THEY WERE TO SUCCESS WHEN THEY GAVE UP."

—THOMAS EDISON

I WANT TO HELP PEOPLE WHO ARE STRUGGLING WITH DEPRESSION
JAMIE TWORKOWSKI

School bored me. I liked seeing my friends, and I liked the girls, of course. But I didn't like the work itself. I was always doodling and daydreaming, always thinking about the future.

I can't say I was daydreaming about someday starting—or running—a nonprofit. But I was always a sensitive kid; I always felt things deeply. My first serious girlfriend struggled with depression, and while I didn't really understand it, I wanted to help.

So even though I ended up in a six-figure job as a sales rep at Hurley, I was so passionate about my project To Write Love on Her Arms that I quit to work on it full-time. A lot of people were baffled. Who quits a job like that to run a MySpace page? That's what it looked like at the time, but I just had the sense that something was happening and it was too special to walk away from. TWLOHA felt important, and it was fun. It still is—it breaks the rules of the average nonprofit. We don't talk about money and fund-raising all the time. We use creativity to reach out to people; we connect.

I went with my gut. My mom would tell you that TWLOHA is everything I've learned, everything I know and care about, under one roof. It's opened amazing doors, to media outlets I never expected and even awards, like the mtvU Good Woodie Award, which I won in 2009. I'm the only nonmusician to even be nominated. I'll never forget that night, or the passion and dedication of our audience that the award represents.

Now, though, I'm looking to the future again. I'm incredibly grateful for what my life has become, but I want to share it with someone. I want a family of my own, and I want to write. I'm still looking ahead, still dreaming big. I can't wait to see what happens next.

- -

Jamie Tworkowski is the founder of To Write Love on Her Arms, a nonprofit organization that aims to present hope for people struggling with addiction, depression, self-injury, and thoughts of suicide. To learn more, visit twloha.com.

I want to build my mom

the most amazing house so
she CAN finally have the home
she deserves.

I WANT TO FOIL A ROBBERY.

BE THE HERO. SHAKE HANDS WITH THE MAYOR. :)

BEFORE I DIE I WANT TO MEET THE NYC POLICE OFFICER WHO DELIVERED ME IN MY PARENTS' BATHROOM BECAUSE THERE WAS NO TIME TO GET TO THE HOSPITAL.

I WANT TO CRASH 50 PARTIES IN 50 STATES.

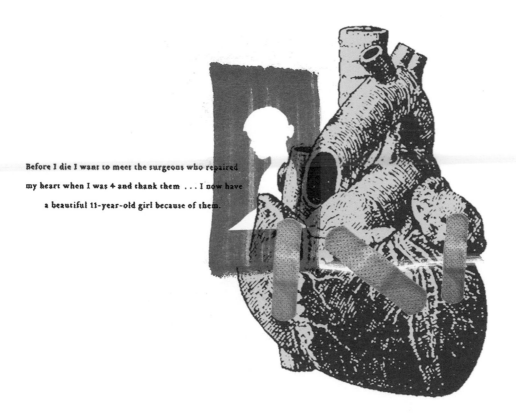

Before I die I want to meet the surgeons who repaired my heart when I was 4 and thank them . . . I now have a beautiful 11-year-old girl because of them.

THROW THE MOST BADASS PARTY EVER

There seems to be a common formula to the legendary parties you see in *Animal House, Old School, Dazed and Confused, Superbad,* and all the other college party movies. In the fall of 2009 we attempted to crack the code by filling a ranch in San Luis Obispo, California, with four hundred coeds from the neighboring town and convincing nineties rap superstars Naughty by Nature to come perform in a giant skate bowl. Six hundred kids showed up. By 1:00 A.M. Treach and Vin Rock of NBN were lifting me on top of a keg. The rest is blurry. Dave ran off naked. At one point a geeky freshman kid brought down the house by freestyle rapping about gangbangs and girls. It was our real-life college party movie. We found Dave naked in a field the next day. He was sunburned. —Duncan

DUNCAN AND DAVE PARTY WITH VIN ROCK AND TREACH FROM
NAUGHTY BY NATURE, SEPTEMBER 2009.

I WAN
SWIM IN

T TO
JELL-O.

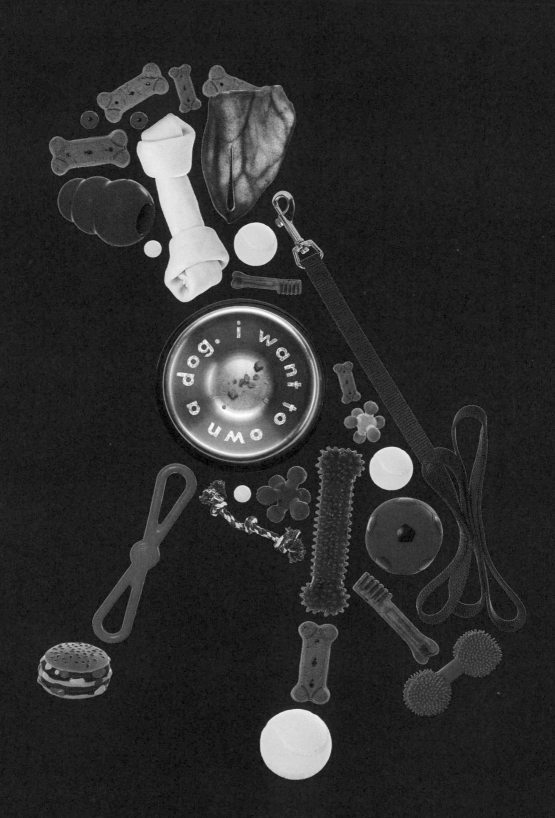

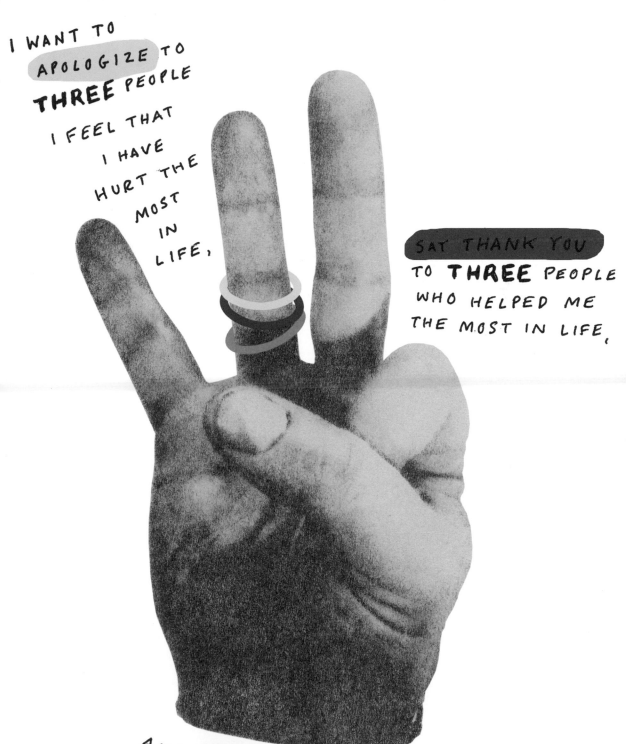

I WANT TO APOLOGIZE TO THREE PEOPLE I FEEL THAT I HAVE HURT THE MOST IN LIFE,

SAY THANK YOU TO THREE PEOPLE WHO HELPED ME THE MOST IN LIFE,

AND RECONNECT WITH THREE PEOPLE I THOUGHT I WOULD NEVER SEE AGAIN.

I WANT TO ROW ACROSS THE ATLANTIC
TORI HOLMES

I'm such an average Joe. Anyone who grew up with me in my small hometown in Alberta would have described me that way—I'm five feet two inches, with strawberry blond hair, and come from a pretty normal family. In high school I was kind of an overachiever, playing every sport and hanging out with every group. The truth was, I was a master of disguise. No one knew—I didn't know—that I was severely dyslexic until almost the end of my time in high school. For years I had just been learning how to learn, hiding the fact that I thought I was stupid. I was very good at achieving, but I had incredibly low self-esteem.

I think that was the real motivator behind my trip with Paul in 2005–2006. I went out there with the thought, "If I can do this, I can do anything—I can teach myself to not be stupid." You know that Robert Frost poem about the two roads diverging in a yellow wood? I'd always wanted to take that other road. Getting into a tiny rowboat and crossing the Atlantic, with just one other person to rely on for almost three months, was my other road.

Just getting to the boat was an ordeal itself. You have to sit down and think, "Am I selfish enough to do this?" You have to look your parents in the eye and tell them that you'll be risking your life, that there is no Plan B out there—you either finish or you almost definitely die.

My parents didn't really understand, but they were willing to support me. But when you wake up after just an hour and a half of sleep to pull the midnight to 2:00 A.M. rowing shift, and it's so dark you can't see the hand in front of your face, and you step out of the cabin and just freeze in terror because the ocean is so big and dark and you're so alone, your parents aren't there to help you. No one is—your partner needs to rest, so he's inside the cabin. Even if the boat capsizes, he can't come out to see if you're okay, or you'll just both end up lost at sea.

One night I watched as a wave rose up and curled over our six-foot-tall cabin and hit me right in the face. It was like being attacked by a wild animal. I went over the side, and all Paul saw was my feet going into the white wash. He couldn't turn the boat around or he'd risk his own life, too, so he had to watch and wait. I was harnessed to the boat, as always, and somehow I pulled myself back in.

But I'd been thrown so hard—I'd hit the water and the bottom of the boat—that, though I didn't know it at the time, I'd broken several ribs and bruised my gallbladder. I was puking up blood, and the pain was indescribable.

We had a satellite phone, which didn't always work, but we managed to reach a friend who was a nursing student at the time. She talked me through the first-aid kit we had. Somehow she figured out that my unrelenting nausea would be helped if I ate toothpaste. I ate a whole tube.

What kept me going, though, what kept me alive, was my dad. The night before that awful shift, he'd sent me a text on the satellite phone, and I swear his words saved my life.

My dad and I have always had a special bond. The row was especially hard for him because he was working in a mine in the Northwest Territories and couldn't even follow our progress online—he was underground, cut off from everything. But one night he woke up with an overwhelming vision of me drowning. He went to the main office of the mine and sent me this message: "Push through the pain, face the fear to Valhalla and back, you're a Viking!"

And just a few hours later I'd been thrown from the boat and I thought I was going to die from injuries I couldn't even really diagnose; I was lying in the cabin, vomiting and in incredible pain. But I kept repeating those words. And after a while I realized, "If I don't get up and row, I'll be out here even longer." So I ate that toothpaste. I got up (and vomited again) and got back to rowing.

For three or four weeks, twelve hours a day, I rowed through the pain. It was like watching someone else—I just disassociated from it. And I kept repeating those words my dad had sent: "Push through the pain, face the fear to Valhalla and back, you're a Viking!" There wasn't a Plan B. I hadn't gone out there to die.

I didn't think I'd see my dad at the end of the race; he couldn't get the time off work. But the morning we came in, he was there. He'd gotten up at 5:00 a.m. just to watch us come over the horizon. Seeing him on the shore was the most emotional moment of my life.

It wasn't anything supernatural, the way he'd saved me. It was just the connection between a parent and his child. I was all the way on the other side of the world, but my dad could feel my danger, and he had the instinct to protect and help. I learned so much about myself on that trip, and every day I carry the quiet confidence that comes from knowing what my limits really are. But through that harrowing time, it was my dad whose strength got me through. I borrowed his strength to survive.

- -

In 2006, at the age of twenty-one, Tori Holmes became the youngest woman to row across an ocean when she and her partner, Paul Gleeson, crossed the Atlantic in a twenty-four-foot boat in eighty-five days. She and Paul recorded their experiences in <u>Crossing the Swell</u>, published in 2009.

"IT WAS ALL A DREAM."

—THE NOTORIOUS B.I.G.

I WANT TO HAVE MY FIRST KISS

I want to convince the person I love the most — my best friend my boyfriend my everything — that life isn't all about making money. The love we share is worth the sacrifice. That happiness has no dollar $ign.

I want to Model
In New York! :)

#42:

SPEND A NIGHT IN JAIL

We left the county jail at 5:05 this morning. Last night we tried to cross off "#50: Streak a Stadium and Get Away with It." We did not get away with it. A dozen local police officers tackled us to the ground, put us in handcuffs, and threw us into the paddy wagon. Then they picked up drunks, deadbeats, and other eccentrics, who didn't love us. Naked strangers don't make the best cellmates.

Our one phone call was to Handsome Brad, our friend and the director of our documentary and TV show. He laughed and said he'd try to figure something out. Brad eventually bailed us out and we danced in the rain like Andy Dufresne escaping Shawshank. Our fines weren't cheap, but we were free . . . at least until we attempt #50 again. —Dave

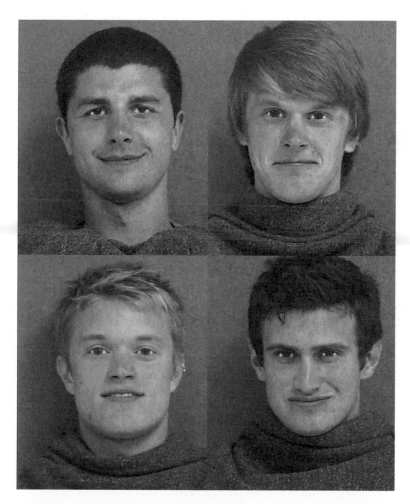

BEN, JONNIE, DUNCAN, AND DAVE'S
COUNTY JAIL MUG SHOTS, JULY 2010.

I want to find my unrelated

I want to take a year and grow *everything* I eat.

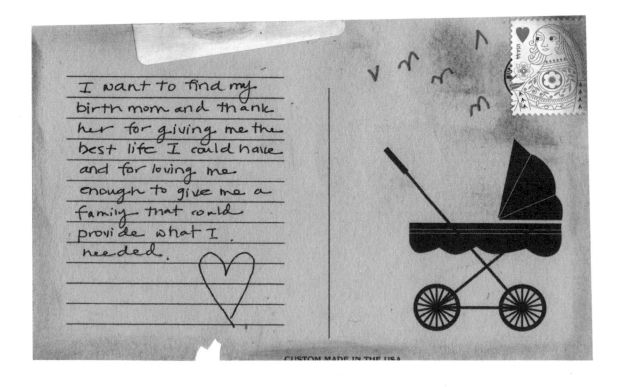

I want to find my birth mom and thank her for giving me the best life I could have and for loving me enough to give me a family that could provide what I needed.

"I'M LIVIN' LIFE RIGHT NOW, MAN.
AND THIS IS WHAT I'MA DO TILL IT'S OVER."

—DRAKE

I WANT TO CLIMB THE SEVEN SUMMITS BEFORE I TURN SEVENTEEN

JOHNNY STRANGE

I just urinated into a bottle and drank it. To stay alive.

It's late at night and the ground under me and my friends shakes with the hooves of huge deer running in the darkness. I'm at the bottom of the Grand Canyon, eighteen hundred feet down, and it's a hot, beautiful night in the desert. We BASE-jumped down to this valley just this morning, the most amazing jump I've ever done. But the plan had been to hike back out and drive away—maybe a four-hour trip.

Instead, over twelve hours have passed. We're stuck. The path we thought we'd take to hike out of here wasn't where we thought it was. We don't have any climbing equipment, and though we calmly tried scaling the rock all day, we kept getting turned back.

Oh, and we're not supposed to be here. This part of the Grand Canyon isn't actually open to visitors. So no one's looking for us, either.

By the end of the morning we were dehydrated, and tonight we've had to drink our own urine. It's awful, but it's better than dying.

Just a couple years ago I climbed Everest, one of the many peaks I've scaled in my nineteen years. I know that above all, you stay calm. My friends are experienced hikers and jumpers, too, and we make it through the night without panicking.

At first light we get up to try again. We're grabbing cactus and trying to eat it. We're still starving and thirsty.

Most of the climbing experience I have is on ice and snow, so the desert heat is a switch for me. The guys and I stick together and take it one rock, one vertical foot, at a time. I'm not thinking too much; I'm just getting this done.

It takes all day, but one of the guys finally finds a way out. He climbs ahead and gets to our car, then turns around and carefully climbs back down to bring the rest of us some water, which gives us the strength to follow him back to the top. It's the best water we've ever had.

My whole goal with everything I do is to bring more awareness to the issues I care about—I go out and do something big so that kids, people, will pay attention. They'll see something crazy I've done on YouTube, and then maybe they'll follow the link about ending genocide or fighting Parkinson's.

- -

Johnny Strange is the youngest person to have climbed the Seven Summits, all of which he scaled by the age of seventeen. He grew up in California and is currently taking time off from USC to travel the world raising awareness about genocide and Parkinson's disease through his videos of extreme sports adventures. To check out Johnny in action, visit his YouTube page.

I want to tell my parents that I Love Them.

I want to take

a cute girl

to the

moon.

i want

to be
SOMEBODY

I WANT TO SAVE A LIFE
MEAGAN McCARTHY

During my freshman year at college, a strange thing happened—which led to an amazing thing happening. All week I had been waking up at 3:00 A.M., exactly. I rarely wake up in the middle of the night, and it was really starting to annoy me! Friday morning, sure enough, I woke up at 3:00.

I got up to go wash my face in the communal dorm bathroom, and when I walked in all I saw was blood.

Of course my first thought was that someone was seriously injured, so I started checking the bathroom stalls and the showers. When I got to the last shower I found a girl with blood on her, sobbing.

I immediately sat down next to her, and before I could say anything she had wrapped her arms around me, holding on for dear life. When I asked her if she was hurt she just held out her wrists. She had been cutting herself.

I'd taken some nursing classes, and I could see that her cuts weren't that deep. She'd bled a lot, but I didn't think she needed to go to the hospital. So I ran back to my room and grabbed a huge first-aid kit and my favorite teddy bear. While I cleaned out and bandaged her cuts, she held on to my teddy bear and told me that an hour before, her boyfriend had broken up with her. He had told her that she wasn't good enough. It absolutely broke my heart.

I sat there with this girl hugging me, both of us covered in blood, for almost three hours. She told me about her life, and I told her about mine. I told her about my first real relationship and how I ended up in court with the guy because he'd threatened to kill me. I told her what I learned—that you have to make yourself happy before you can make anyone else happy.

After about an hour of sharing, before I said good-bye and got her to a safe place, she said, "I wasn't planning on leaving this bathroom alive. Thank you, because you saved my life."

Hearing that was the most unreal, dreamlike thing I have ever experienced. This was why I had been getting up at 3:00 A.M. all week. Someone knew that this girl was going to need help—my help. I am a firm believer that all your experiences in life, no matter how hard, happen for a reason. They make you stronger, smarter, braver. I was supposed to be there, and I was lucky to be there.

And I got to cross off my list #8: Save a life.

Meagan McCarthy is a student at the University of Arizona at Tucson, majoring in communications and sports management. Her "What to do before I die" list has forty-three items—so far—and she's crossed off nineteen of them. Her biggest dream is to help her parents out with the cost of her education.

#95:

PLAY BALL WITH THE PRESIDENT

This was added to the list in 2008. I was paying $200 a month to live in my friend's laundry room. On my door was a poster of President Obama from *Rolling Stone* magazine. There he was, smiling shyly at me every morning as I left for class. Reading *The Audacity of Hope* gave me the idea: If Obama could make it to the White House, why couldn't we?

It took two years to accomplish. We worked tirelessly petitioning senators, congressmen, and other public figures for help. Nothing worked. It was the president himself who finally made it happen. He surprised us on a tour of the White House basketball courts with a short game. He said he'd overturned the press team's initial decision not to host the game because he liked that we helped people. Greatest honor of my life. —Jonnie

JONNIE, DAVE, PRESIDENT OBAMA, DUNCAN, AND BEN ON
THE WHITE HOUSE BASKETBALL COURTS, MARCH 2010.

I want to share my artwork with The World.

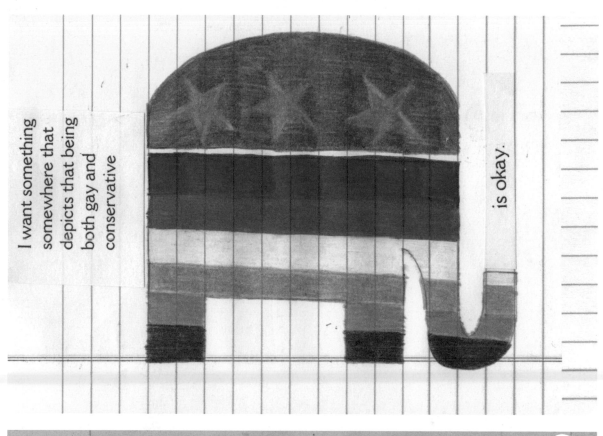

I want something somewhere that depicts that being both gay and conservative

is okay.

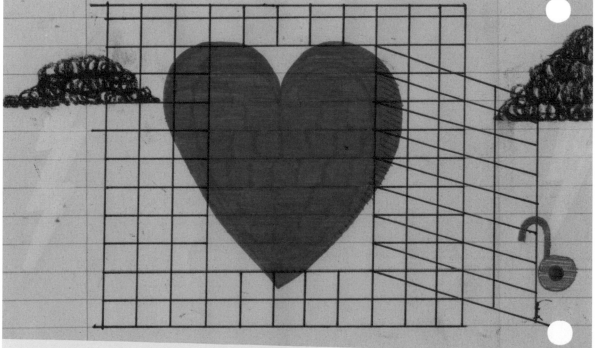

I want to see my sister out of her emotionally abusive relationship.

I WANT TO
BE A MAN.

I WANT TO FARM MY OWN LAND.

I want to go to a cemetery and put a flower on every grave.

I WANT TO MAKE
FOOTPRINTS ON THE MOON.

I WANT TO APOLOGIZE FOR PEEING ON JENNA'S DOOR
DAVE LINGWOOD

The opportunity to work as an assistant guide in Namibia at my uncle's Wild Dog Safari—my dream job—had landed in my lap. Watching people's reactions when they spotted lions roaming through the tall grass for the first time was awesome, and despite the fact I had to rise at 5:00 A.M. to make my boss coffee, I loved my job. We should note—a morning person, I am not.

I guess the early-morning coffee fetching got to me eventually. After a three-month stint in Africa I found myself in Lethbridge, Alberta, enrolled in university. Not exactly thrilled at the thought of swapping safari tours and elephants for a school in small-town-prairie Canada, I decided to be "That Guy" you see in every college movie. I had a fully stocked bar and the sickest sound system in my dorm.

Hour twenty-two of college life: I woke up to a security guard nudging me in the dorm foyer. I was naked with a small towel wrapped around me and apparently had forgotten the entry code to the building. After kindly thanking the guard, I decided to have a shower and perhaps a quick nap before my first class. When I looked in the mirror I saw that—to my surprise—a flaming shooter had burned off my left eyebrow.

So it continued. Five to seven nights a week I was stumbling drunk. After eight months existing on twelve-packs and cafeteria food, my badonkadonk was so large that my nickname, D. Lo, had stuck. I was forty-five pounds heavier than when I arrived. My grades were terrible and continued to get worse. I had to start withdrawing from courses.

"Jenna, I'm so sorry for peeing on your door. I have cleaned everything around it and even shampooed the carpet. I'm so sorry. —Dave." Messages like this became more frequent. When my dry-erase scribble became recognizable by everyone in my dorm, I knew my drinking was out of hand.

The second semester was in full swing. I was depressed and battling severe social anxiety. Talking to others was really uncomfortable—I constantly felt like I was squirming in my own skin. Deep down I began to realize that this behavior was surface noise for what was really going on underneath. I needed to do something about it; I just didn't know what.

When I got home my friend Olivier greeted me with "Holy shit, you're fat." A dapper East Indian dude, Olivier was the kind of guy who would host a party, break a beer bottle over his head with a smile, and then wake up the next morning at six to give a speech to a board of directors on social change. He answers the phone in a rush: "Hey, man. I just got back from a fifteen-mile run and I'm about to sit down and compose the musical score for this new screenplay I'm working on. But what's up?"

His overachieving personality could have been overwhelming if he weren't such a G. Olivier became my very own Tony Robbins. Disclaimer: Every so often, the Olivier Tony Robbins may have a few beers and try to fight you—I hear the real one does not.

One night we spent eight hours talking. For the first time, I opened up and told him that my life was unraveling. I was depressed and miserable. Olivier shook his head and nailed it with zero pity: "It sounds like you just wasted an entire year of your life." And I had.

He fired questions at me: "Where do you want to be in ten years? What does that look like? Who do you most admire? Who blows your mind?"

For the first time in years, dreams, passion, inspiration, and a faint surge of hope came over me. It was a dull sensation, but I liked it. There was something to look forward to in my future. We sat in an '81 Volvo all night. I can still hear the song by Broken Social Scene playing on repeat. By 3:00 A.M., I had a page of notes and Olivier was assigning homework. I was going to get my grades up, I would go after what made me happy, and of course I had to go for a run—stat.

Olivier kept me in check and made sure that everything I committed to or said I wanted to do, I did—small steps in the right direction. The first year of my college journey was selfish. I was slacking, lazy, and running away. Olivier's "You have no one to blame but yourself" model slapped me in the face, and it finally hit me that I could choose the life I wished to lead. If I wanted to change, it would need to come from within. By the end of first semester of second year I was earning A's and B's—the highest grades I'd ever gotten. I taught break dancing three days a week, and I lost all but my freshman fifteen. Most important, I was happy, passionate, and excited about my future rather than worried. It was a Tuesday in February I got a phone call about a new opportunity. It was Jonnie, arranging a meeting with some guys from back home about a film project.

- -

Dave Lingwood is ready to go get dinner. He's going to pick you up in an hour. He saw on Yelp that there was a taco place down on Lincoln that is supposed to be amazing. Be there soon. Dave is also one of the four founders of The Buried Life. He likes break dancing and eating (obviously).

I want to finally say good-bye to my four friends who were killed in a car accident.

I want to Witness A Miracle

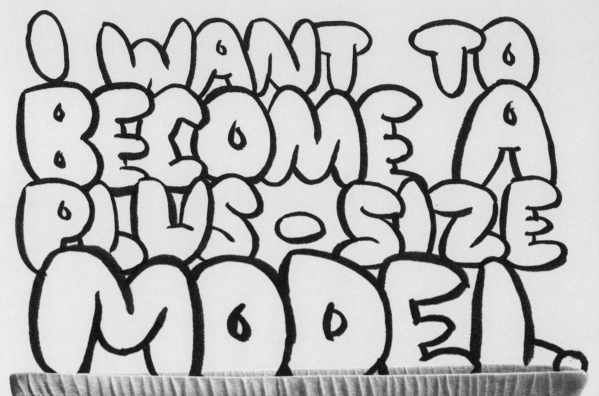

I WANT TO BECOME A PLUS-SIZE MODEL

TO SHOW YOUNG GIRLS THAT BEAUTY ISN'T A SIZE 6 OR SMALLER.

The POWER of Your Subconscious Mind

Joseph Murphy

D.R.S., D.D., Ph.D., LL.D.
Fellow of the Andhra Research
University of India

I WANT TO READ SOMEONE'S MIND.

BANTAM BOOKS
NEW YORK · TORONTO · LONDON · SYDNEY · AUCKLAND

#59:

ASK OUT THE GIRL OF YOUR DREAMS

Asking out Taylor Swift was an epic undertaking involving fake country music stars, glued sideburns, security hopping, and a secret note. You can do a quick search on Google to see how Duncan did it. —Dave

TAYLOR SWIFT AT THE CMT MUSIC AWARDS, TWO HOURS
BEFORE DUNCAN SNUCK INSIDE AND ASKED HER OUT.
NASHVILLE, TENNESSEE, JUNE 2010.

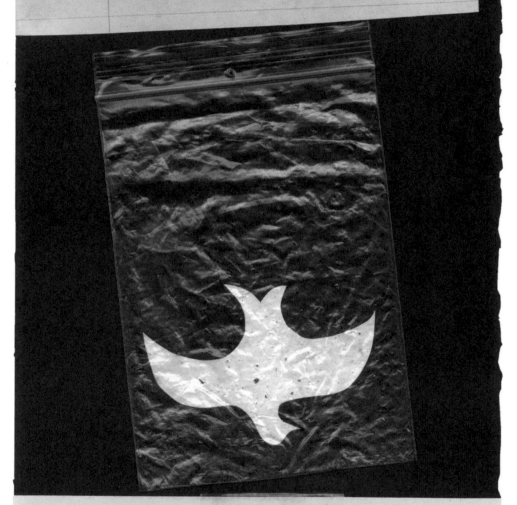

I want to rappel off Mount Rushmore.

I WANT ALL MY BUDDIES TO MAKE IT BACK

FROM AFGHANISTAN AND IRAQ

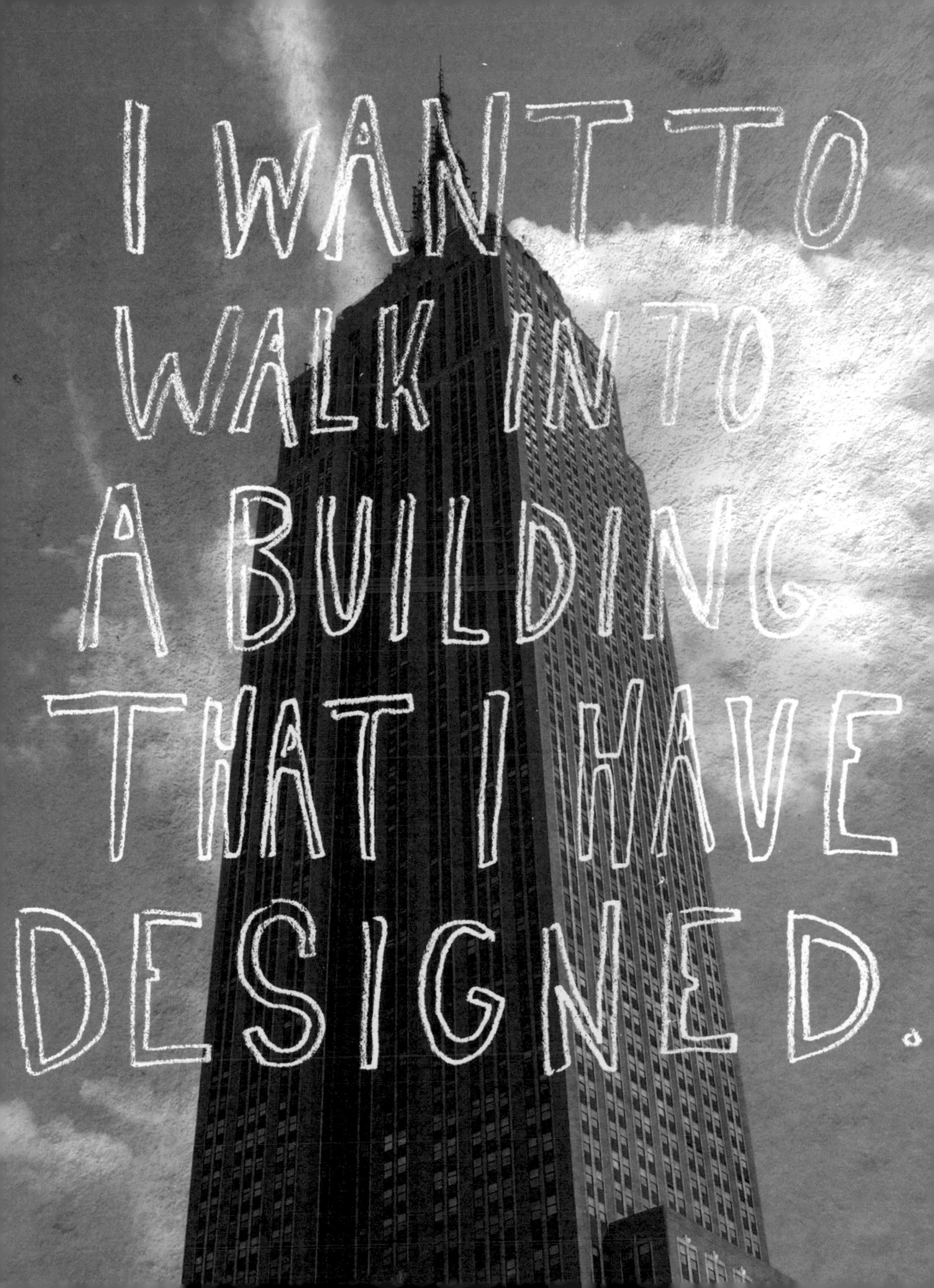
I WANT TO
WALK INTO
A BUILDING
THAT I HAVE
DESIGNED.

I WANT

NOT TO
BE SCARED

TO LET MYSELF

FALL
HEAD OVER
HEELS
IN LOVE
AGAIN.

I WANT TO WALK AWAY

FROM AN EXPLOSION

(IN SLOW MOTION)

#88: SURVIVE ON A DESERTED ISLAND

We all read *Lord of the Flies* in high school and daydreamed about being one of the kids in the book. What would it be like? How would we survive?

In the fall of 2010 we flew to Rarotonga to find out. We were dropped blindfolded a few hundred meters from the beach. We had nothing with us but the clothes on our backs and one item each: a snorkel (Dave), a flashlight (Ben), a pot (Jonnie), and a machete (me).

I remember watching the full moon rise three days later and thinking, "This is what I came for." I was delirious from lack of sleep and dehydration. All we'd consumed in seventy-two hours was coconut juice. But I was happy. We were the Lost Boys, Tom Hanks in *Cast Away*; we were men! And all it took was a trip to the middle of the Pacific. —Duncan

DAVE, JONNIE, BEN, AND DUNCAN ARRIVE BACK TO CIVILIZATION
AFTER FOUR DAYS WITHOUT FOOD, WATER, OR SUPPLIES.
OCTOBER 2010.

I want to have a boat named after me.

I want me and my family to become

American citizens.

"NEVER TELL ME THE SKY
IS THE LIMIT WHEN THERE ARE
FOOTPRINTS ON THE MOON."

—ANONYMOUS

I **WANT** to go to a city where NOBODY knows me...

...AND ACT like a COMPLETELY DIFFERENT PERSON.

I want to get my parents

out of debt.

I WANT TO FEEL WHAT IT'S LIKE TO USE MY LEGS.

I WANNA POP SOME TOAST
JONNIE PENN

Alexander the Great conquered the known world when he was twenty-two. S. E. Hinton wrote *The Outsiders* at fifteen. Mark Zuckerberg started Facebook at nineteen.

When you're young you often feel a need to justify your ambitions. I still feel that way sometimes. I apologize for things I want to create or do if they don't make sense to my friends or family.

Every time I look through the pages of this book, I get the same feeling I got the first time I jumped aboard Bedadu with Ben, Dave, and Duncan in the summer of 2006: No apologies. We're doing this.

I still find myself boxing up good ideas out of fear here and there.

My inspiration comes out of the community that The Buried Life has become: a place for people who like to feel crazy once in a while.

But how better to grow? Hope is crazy. Love is crazy. Crazy is how Alex, Susan, and Mark became Alexander the Great, S. E. Hinton, and Mark Zuckerberg.

Maybe crazy isn't such a bad thing to be. I think I might start unpacking.

Jonnie Penn is one of six kids and Duncan's brother. He attended McGill University in Montreal and represented Canada at the International Debate Tournaments at Oxford University. He is very serious and does not like jokes. Scientifically, he is the most handsome of the Buried Life guys.

I WANT TO BE ROUNDHOUSE KICKED BY CHUCK NORRIS. IT WOULD HURT BUT BE SO WORTH IT.

"SOONER OR LATER THE MAN WHO WINS
IS THE MAN WHO THINKS HE CAN."
—NAPOLEON HILL

I WANT TO CREW WITH THE
SEA SHEPHERDS AND HELP
SAVE THE WORLD'S OCEANS.

I WANT TO FIND MY MOM A BOYFRIEND.*

* AND I WANT HIM TO TREAT HER RIGHT, TOO !

Della Howell-Graham ▶
Stephen Childs

I want to be sure that my husband knows just how much I love him...that there is nothing else in the entire world that has or ever could make me even the slightest bit as happy as he makes me every single second.

28 days ago · Comment · Like · Dislike · Reconsider · Fast Forward · Contemplate in Silence

   You and 814 other people like this.

Della Howell-Graham ▶
Stephen Childs

I want to be sure that my husband knows just how much I love him...that there is nothing else in the entire world that has or ever could make me even the slightest

PROTEST SOMETHING

I want to do this more often.

    I began my journey on The Buried Life as a pissed-off kid, and not that much has changed. There is so much wrong with the world and so much that can be done by standing up to it. Creativity is key. Whatever you believe in, do your research and make yourself heard. If it's not working, try again. —Jonnie

THE OIL'S CAPPED BUT THE SWIMMING STILL SUCKS.

BEN, DUNCAN, DAVE, AND JONNIE ARRIVE AT THE DO SOMETHING AWARDS COVERED IN OIL TO PROTEST BRITISH PETROLEUM'S SLOW RESPONSE TO THE DEVASTATING OIL SPILL THEY CAUSED, JULY 2010.

I WANT TO SEE MY
SISTER
OVERCOME HER
ANXIETY. SHE'S ONLY
18 AND HAS
BARELY LEFT
THE HOUSE
IN 4 YEARS.

I WANT TO ACT (INSIDE A COMPUTER)
BING GORDON

Mine is a sort of bad teacher–good teacher story.

In college I took a course called Decision-making and Psychology. For a big project I wanted to figure out the math of how people choose a date for the prom. That kind of real-life decision-making really appealed to me. But so did the scientific process, so I interviewed people, I tested outliers—guy-to-guy, guy-to-pet, student-to-teacher—to determine ratings.

The assistant professors gave me a zero. I was shocked. I figured that they thought I'd missed something in the math. But it was my topic, the prom. They didn't think I was taking the class seriously. I was stuck with the zero. Clearly my sense of what was popular decision-making math was different—but, I was still convinced, better—than theirs.

Years later, in grad school, I had an opposite classroom experience. About ten minutes before the end of class one day, Professor Peter Keen changed the subject, and my life. He said, "Let's talk about something that's actually important. You might be broke right now," he told us, "but what would you do if money were no object?"

I'd been thinking about my own idea for a while. I wanted to create a kind of adult Disneyland that you lived and created characters in, all inside a computer. I'd been an actor for a few years, and while I liked re-creating stories, it had always frustrated me that as an actor you have no control over the pace of the story, or the outcome. Or the other actors.

So that's what I told them. And the classroom just fell completely silent. Everyone thought this was really embarrassing, and they all felt sorry for me.

Afterward, Professor Keen pulled me aside. He told me he had another student who'd said something similar about a computer idea and suggested maybe I should get together with him. That guy was Trip Hawkins, who founded EA a few years later. He brought me on board to help fulfill the vision of software as a new entertainment medium, which produced culture-changing simulations like John Madden Football, Need for Speed, and the biggest hit of them all, The Sims.

Professor Keen might have thought I was crazy, but he didn't assume I was joking. And I wasn't—The Sims is based on the decision-making math I tested (and scored a zero on) in college. To date, it's sold 100 million copies.

William "Bing" Gordon was a founding member and chief creative officer of Electronic Arts (EA), the video game company behind The Sims and many other products. He is now a venture capitalist with Kleiner Perkins Caufield & Byers and serves on the boards of Amazon and Zynga.

I WANT TO GO ON AN ADVENTURE WITH MY BROTHERS JONNIE AND DUNCAN AND MY LITTLE SISTER—TAKE A ROAD TRIP, OR BACKPACK THROUGH EUROPE, OR VISIT A DESERT ISLAND, OR SEE THE GULF ISLANDS.

I want to save
someone who is
trapped in a
burning building.

1. B. Murray

2. D. Aykroyd

I want to meet
the Ghostbusters.

3. H. Ramis

4. E. Hudson

#92:

LEARN HOW TO SURF

Every time I go surfing I'm reminded that I don't need a list of things to do before I die. Why try to play basketball with the president (#95) or make a TV show (#53) when I can spend hours of total peace alone in the water? When I'm back on land my old ambitions inevitably creep up, but while I'm in the water I'm happy. And that's all the list is ever supposed to make us. —Duncan

DUNCAN, BEN, DAVE, AND JONNIE HOLD PRO SURFER
MARY OSBORNE, VENTURA, CALIFORNIA, AUGUST 2007.

I want to fall in love one more time. Even though I am married to the last person I fell in love with. Even though I am committed to the marriage.

BEFORE I DIE

I WANT TO FIND

THE GIRL I FELL

IN LOVE WITH ON

A SHORT FLIGHT.

I WANT TO STOP CUTTING
LEXIE LINDSKOG

I always felt guilty; I was always doing something wrong or hurting some-one. The only way to balance things out was to write LOSER or FAIL on my arms. And hide—hide away from everyone.

At first I used bobby pins, so small and easy to find. I'd break one in half and rip off that little protective plastic covering that makes the tip dull. But it wasn't super sharp, either, and the marks I'd make on my skin were more like etches than cuts. I didn't bleed. So it didn't really count as cutting.

It wasn't long, though, before etching wasn't enough to break through the guilt and the numbness. I'd take a really hot shower, so that my skin would be a little numb, and then go to work with a much more effective tool—a box cutter. At first the etchings were enough, but now I wanted to bleed. I wanted it to hurt. I would make cuts on parts of my body that were easier to hide with clothes—my upper arms, my chest, my legs. I would lie in bed and just feel the sting of the fresh wounds.

I still have FAIL scarred on my leg. But some of the failures saved my life. I didn't succeed in killing myself, though I tried more than once. And though I'd become a master of my masks, showing only parts of myself to certain people, I never really succeeded in hiding completely. My closest friends reached out—said they were worried, called the cops when I was sending them scary text messages about how they wouldn't have to deal with me anymore. My family had been sending me to counselors for years, trying to help me manage how intense my feelings always seemed to be.

But I was hidden from myself. I was refusing to face the truth: that I have borderline personality disorder. I kept thinking that I could just control my behavior and that nothing really had to change. Still, the disorder was mak-ing it impossible to function normally, and by running from the diagnosis I was only making things worse.

If anything was going to change, I had to really reach out. I had kept myself from cutting for about three weeks when I sent an e-mail to the Buried Life guys. As soon as I pressed SEND I couldn't believe what I'd done—and after that, nothing was the same.

It wasn't the fact that they responded that changed my life—it was the fact that I'd finally reached out. Meeting Ben and the guys changed everything.

- -

Lexie Lindskog lives in Rochester, Minnesota, where she works with her local chapter of the National Alliance on Mental Illness (NAMI), raising awareness about borderline personality disorder, cutting, and depression. Lexie has not cut herself since July 2010. For more about her story and her work, find Lexie on Facebook and Twitter.

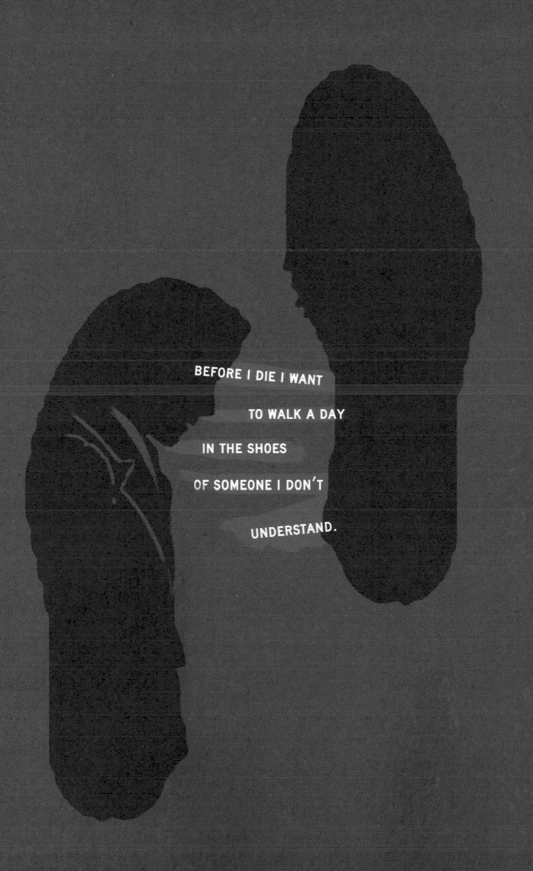

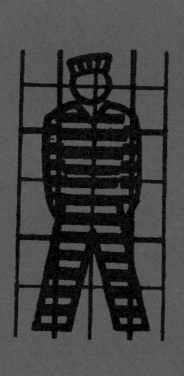

I want my dad to be on the other side of the bars without the orange jumpsuit.

I WANT MY PARENTS TO SAY,

"THAT'S MY DAUGHTER."

"IT'S NEVER TOO LATE TO BE
WHAT YOU MIGHT HAVE BEEN."

—GEORGE ELIOT

I want to
toboggan
down

a double
black
diamond.

I

no longer

want to

be afraid

of the dark.

"STAY HUNGRY. STAY FOOLISH."
—STEWART BRAND

I want to go around the world in 80 days in a hot-air balloon!

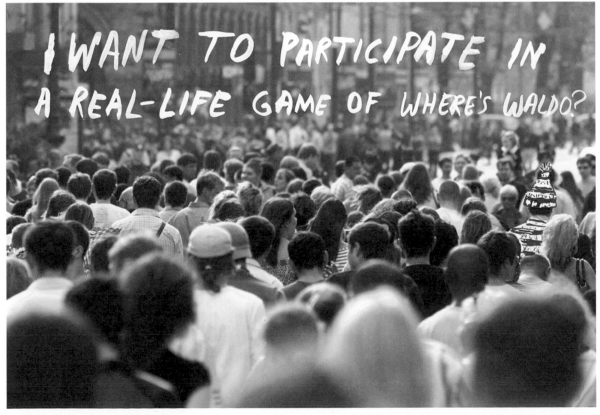

i want to be

COMPLETELY

and...

BLISSFULLY

:) HAPPY :)

I WANT TO CREATE AND NAME A NEW COLOR CRAYON.

I want to make a mark.

THANK YOU

Our most sincere thanks to all of our friends and family; to our hometown of Victoria, British Columbia; to the few special individuals who taught us that dreams can become a reality; to the hardworking artists who gave the project form and a structure; to the young people around the world who fuel The Buried Life. We're honored to have been able to make this journey with you.

BEN, DAVE, DUNCAN, JONNIE

Hope you enjoyed our book. Mischief managed.